Dark Web Reality

Truth, Terror, and the Tunnels of the Internet's Hidden World

Table of Contents

Introduction

In the modern digital age, where the internet governs everything from social interaction to financial transactions, there exists a layer far removed from the daily clicks and scrolls of the average user. This layer is mysterious, hidden, and often misunderstood—it is the dark web. To most, the phrase conjures images of faceless hackers, underground marketplaces, and unspeakable crimes. Hollywood films and media headlines have painted the dark web as a lawless digital frontier teeming with danger, deceit, and illicit dealings. But the truth is far more complex, nuanced, and—at times—even strangely noble.

The dark web is not a single website or a solitary platform. It is a segment of the internet that is not indexed by traditional search engines and requires specific software, like the Tor browser, to access. While it certainly hosts illegal activity, it also serves as a critical tool for whistleblowers, activists, and journalists in oppressive regimes who rely on it to communicate safely. It is both a sanctuary for free expression and a breeding ground for criminal enterprise. This duality is what makes the dark web so fascinating—and so important to understand.

Separating fact from fiction is no easy task. There is a great deal of misinformation surrounding the dark web, often fueled by sensationalist media coverage and fictional accounts that blur the line between reality and myth. Stories of hitmen for hire, live-streamed torture sessions, and organ trafficking capture public attention, but how much of it is actually true? What are the real dangers, and where does exaggeration begin? This book aims to peel back the digital curtain and offer an honest, investigative look into what truly happens in the tunnels of the internet's hidden world.

The reason this book matters is simple: understanding the dark web is essential in an age where digital privacy, cybercrime, and information freedom are hotly debated and deeply intertwined. Governments are cracking down on encryption tools, hackers are becoming more sophisticated, and ordinary people are finding themselves affected by leaks and data breaches rooted in dark web activity. Whether you are a cybersecurity enthusiast, a curious reader, or someone concerned about your own online safety, this book is your guide through the shadows. We will explore how the dark web works, who uses it, and why it exists. We will uncover both the darkness and the light—because only by seeing clearly can we navigate safely.

Welcome to Dark Web Reality. Let's begin our journey into the digital underworld.

Chapter 1
The Three Layers of the Internet

When most people think of the internet, they imagine the familiar landscape of search engines, news sites, streaming platforms, and social media—the visible portion that we use every day. But this easily accessible realm, known as the surface web, is just the tip of the iceberg. Beneath it lies an expansive and hidden structure composed of layers that most users never see or even realize exist. These layers—the surface web, deep web, and dark web—each serve different purposes and function in dramatically different ways.

This chapter begins by explaining the structure of the internet in its entirety, breaking it down into these three core components. We will examine how the surface web is indexed and crawled by search engines, how the deep web contains vast amounts of unindexed data like medical records and academic databases, and how the dark web hides behind layers of encryption and anonymity tools like Tor. While the surface web may only account for a small fraction of the actual internet, the deep and dark webs together comprise the majority of online data.

It is essential to understand how these layers interact, overlap, and sometimes blur in function. For example, not all of the deep web is nefarious—some of it is entirely legal and essential to daily life. Similarly, the dark web is not solely a criminal playground. These distinctions are often misunderstood due to media misrepresentation and a lack of public education.

In the pages ahead, we will clarify these misconceptions, laying a factual foundation for understanding the hidden corners of the web. Before we can navigate the tunnels of the dark web, we must first understand how deep the internet really goes.

Surface, Deep, and Dark Web Explained

The internet, as most people know it, is merely a fraction of the vast digital landscape that exists. What we access through search engines like Google or Bing—the websites we visit daily, such as news platforms, social media, shopping sites, and blogs—is only the surface. Beneath this familiar layer lies an immense and largely invisible structure of data and activity: the deep web and, further still, the dark web. To grasp the significance and complexity of the dark web, it is vital to first understand the distinctions between these three layers—surface web, deep web, and dark web—and how they fit together in the overall architecture of the internet.

The surface web, also known as the visible or indexed web, consists of websites and pages that are accessible through traditional web browsers and are indexed by search engines. If you can find it by typing a query into Google and clicking a link, it resides on the surface web. Examples include Wikipedia articles, news websites, YouTube videos, Facebook posts, and online shopping portals. Though this is the most familiar part of the internet, it accounts for less than 5% of the total content available online. Its accessibility and visibility make it the most widely used layer, but also the most limited in scope.

Below the surface lies the deep web—a vast portion of the internet that is not indexed by search engines and therefore not easily accessible to the general public. Unlike the surface web, the deep web contains content that is hidden behind paywalls, authentication forms, private databases, and encrypted services. Examples include online banking portals, academic journals, private cloud storage, subscription services like Netflix or research databases, and internal company intranets. Accessing this information typically requires login credentials or direct URLs. Importantly, the deep web is not inherently illicit or dangerous; in fact, it serves legitimate and essential functions across education, healthcare, finance, and government sectors. Its obscurity is often intended to protect privacy and sensitive information.

Venturing further down, we reach the dark web, a subset of the deep web that is intentionally hidden and requires specialized software to access. The most common gateway is the Tor (The Onion Router) network, which anonymizes users and allows access to sites with .onion extensions. Unlike the deep web, where users may still leave digital footprints traceable to their identities or IP addresses, the dark web is designed for maximum anonymity—both for users and for website operators. This cloak of secrecy makes it a haven for privacy advocates, whistleblowers, and individuals living under oppressive regimes. At the same time, it attracts cybercriminals, black market operators, and others who seek to evade detection by law enforcement or regulatory bodies.

The dark web is most often associated with illegal marketplaces selling drugs, weapons, counterfeit documents, stolen data, and hacking tools. Platforms like Silk Road, AlphaBay, and Hansa gained infamy for enabling such activities before being dismantled by global law enforcement agencies. However, not all dark web activity is criminal. There are forums for political discussion, encrypted email services, journalism outlets like ProPublica's .onion site, and anonymous platforms used by whistleblowers to leak information safely. The dual nature of the dark web—as both a tool for freedom and a shield for crime—adds to its complexity and controversy.

One common misconception is that the dark web and deep web are the same. While both are not indexed by search engines, they are fundamentally different in purpose and access. The deep web is largely benign and functional, while the dark web includes content deliberately hidden and often encrypted to avoid visibility and traceability. Another misconception is that accessing the dark web is in itself illegal. In truth, browsing the dark web is legal in many countries, though participating in illegal activities on it is not. The tools used to access it, like the Tor browser, are open-source and legal technologies used by journalists, activists, and regular citizens concerned about surveillance and data tracking.

The media often dramatizes the dark web as a hellish landscape filled with violent content and sinister actors lurking in every corner. While illegal content certainly exists, such sensationalism can obscure the broader truths and mislead people about what the dark web really is. In reality, the dark web is a tool—a powerful one—that can be used for both good and evil depending on who is wielding it and for what purpose.

Understanding the differences between the surface web, deep web, and dark web is essential to navigating the digital world responsibly. As this book will explore further, the dark web is not simply a place of danger and darkness; it is a complex ecosystem of anonymity, privacy, risk, and resilience. To explore it wisely, we must first understand where it begins, where it ends, and how it fits within the broader internet landscape.

How They Interact

The internet is not a set of isolated layers but rather a dynamic and interconnected ecosystem where the surface web, deep web, and dark web interact more closely than most people realize. These three layers are not separate networks existing in isolation, but extensions of the same global digital infrastructure, differing primarily in terms of accessibility, visibility, and purpose. Understanding how they interact helps us grasp how information flows, how cyber threats propagate, and how digital privacy and security are maintained—or compromised—across the broader internet.

At the top, the surface web functions as the public face of the internet. It's indexed by search engines like Google, Bing, and Yahoo, and includes content such as websites, blogs, news articles, and social media platforms. Most internet users remain within this layer. However, even within surface web platforms, links may lead to deeper parts of the internet. For example, a Google search may bring up a login page for your online banking or email account. Once you sign in, you move from the surface web to the deep web, since the content behind that login page is not publicly indexed or visible.

This is a clear demonstration of interaction between the surface and deep web: one serves as a gateway to the other. Social media is another example. You can see a user's public profile on the surface web, but their private messages, account settings, and hidden content reside within the deep web, accessible only through authenticated sessions. News websites, academic libraries, and subscription-based platforms also operate this way—offering publicly visible landing pages but restricting full content to registered or paying users. The surface web acts as a bridge or access point to the deeper layer, creating an interactive loop between what's seen and what's hidden.

The deep web in turn interacts with the dark web, though in more complex and controlled ways. While the deep web includes private but legitimate services like academic portals, cloud storage, and internal business systems, the dark web is an encrypted subset that's accessed through specific tools like the Tor browser. These services often rely on the same hosting infrastructure and internet backbone as surface and deep web sites, making them technically connected even if functionally segregated. For instance, the Tor network itself operates through volunteer servers distributed across the globe—some of which are also used for surface web traffic anonymization. This shared technical infrastructure means that data packets, whether from surface browsing or a hidden .onion site, may travel through overlapping nodes or routes across the internet.

Interactions between the deep web and dark web are also visible in certain online behaviors. Cybercriminals often exfiltrate sensitive data—such as passwords, medical records, or financial information—from deep web systems (like breached databases) and then sell or leak that data on dark web forums or marketplaces. This creates a functional pipeline: information harvested from the deep web is monetized or exposed through the dark web. Conversely, users may use information obtained on the dark web to launch attacks against deep web targets, such as phishing campaigns using stolen email credentials or malware distribution through compromised academic platforms.

Even the surface web interacts with the dark web, albeit more indirectly. For example, media outlets often report on dark web activity, linking to data leaks or criminal arrests. In some cases, users on the surface web find themselves inadvertently engaging with dark web content through malicious links, phishing schemes, or misinformation campaigns. Law enforcement agencies, cybersecurity firms, and journalists routinely monitor the dark web to identify threats that could spill over into the surface web—such as coordinated disinformation campaigns, doxxing threats, or upcoming cyberattacks.

Furthermore, anonymization tools that originated for dark web access—like Tor or I2P—are now being used across all internet layers. Journalists use Tor to securely transmit information over the deep or surface web. Everyday users use VPNs or private browsers to mask their digital footprints while browsing the surface. This technological interaction blurs the lines between the layers even more, creating a continuum rather than strict borders.

It's also important to note that data flows across all three layers. A piece of information—like a stolen credit card—may originate from a surface web breach, be stored in a deep web repository, and end up being sold on a dark web marketplace. This cycle shows how threats are interconnected and why cybersecurity solutions must address the entire spectrum of the internet, not just the visible parts.

In essence, the surface web, deep web, and dark web are not isolated entities but interconnected components of a single digital universe. Each plays a role in how information is stored, accessed, and protected. Their interactions define the internet's complexity and underscore the importance of understanding the full structure—not just the part we can see. Recognizing these connections helps users better protect themselves and allows governments, businesses, and cybersecurity professionals to build more comprehensive strategies for digital safety and resilience.

Common Misconceptions

The dark web is one of the most misunderstood components of the internet, shrouded in myth, media exaggeration, and a general lack of clarity. While it's true that the dark web can host illicit content and activities, much of what people believe about it is either distorted, oversimplified, or entirely false. These misconceptions not only fuel fear and confusion but also prevent people from understanding the broader structure of the internet and the true nature of privacy, cybersecurity, and digital freedom. In this section, we will explore some of the most common misconceptions surrounding the surface web, deep web, and dark web, and clarify what's fact and what's fiction.

One of the most widespread misconceptions is the belief that the deep web and dark web are the same. In reality, they are two very different parts of the internet. The deep web includes all content that isn't indexed by standard search engines, such as personal emails, private cloud files, banking records, subscription services, and government databases. Most of us interact with the deep web every day when we log into our Gmail accounts or access medical portals. It is entirely legal and forms the backbone of secure digital communication. The dark web, on the other hand, is a small, intentionally hidden subset of the deep web, accessible only through special anonymizing tools like the Tor browser. It is within this encrypted layer that you'll find both pro-privacy services and illicit activities.

Another common myth is that accessing the dark web is inherently illegal. This is not true. Simply visiting a .onion site using a tool like Tor is not a criminal act in most countries. In fact, Tor was originally developed by the U.S. Navy to support anonymous communication and is still used today by journalists, human rights activists, and whistleblowers to avoid surveillance. Legal usage of the dark web includes secure communication, uncensored news access in oppressive countries, and research into cybersecurity threats. What is illegal is engaging in criminal activities on the dark web, such as purchasing drugs, distributing child exploitation materials, or hiring cybercriminals.

A particularly sensational and persistent misconception involves the existence of "Red Rooms", which are rumored to be live-streamed torture or murder sessions where users can pay to influence the victim's fate. This narrative is frequently repeated in horror stories, conspiracy forums, and fictional media, but there is no verified evidence that such sites exist. Most so-called Red Rooms are scams designed to exploit the fears and morbid curiosity of users, often demanding payment and never delivering on the promised (and illegal) content. While the dark web can host disturbing material, the technical and logistical complexity of such operations, combined with the scrutiny of law enforcement, makes the actual existence of Red Rooms highly unlikely.

Similarly, people often assume that the dark web is entirely lawless and immune to regulation, which again is not accurate. While it does offer strong anonymity, law enforcement agencies have had notable success in infiltrating and shutting down dark web marketplaces. Operations like the takedown of Silk Road, AlphaBay, and Hansa involved international cooperation, undercover agents, and digital forensics. Governments are becoming more adept at navigating the dark web, tracking illegal activity, and prosecuting offenders. The idea that one can operate with impunity in this hidden corner of the internet is outdated and misleading.

Another misconception is that the dark web is a large portion of the internet. In reality, the dark web makes up only a tiny fraction of the overall web—estimates suggest less than 0.01%. The deep web, by contrast, is vast, encompassing more than 90% of all internet content. This includes academic databases, legal records, cloud storage, corporate networks, and more. The notion that the dark web is this huge, uncontrollable digital underworld is exaggerated and contributes to public misunderstanding.

Lastly, people often believe that the dark web is only used by criminals, when in fact it also serves as a vital tool for protecting freedom of speech and digital rights. In countries with heavy censorship, dissidents use dark web services to access banned websites, communicate securely, and share critical information without risking arrest or retaliation. Organizations like SecureDrop allow whistleblowers to submit information to journalists without exposing their identity. Even mainstream media outlets like the BBC and ProPublica have launched Tor mirror sites to ensure access to accurate information in restrictive regions.

Understanding and debunking these misconceptions is critical, not only to accurately assess the risks of the dark web but also to appreciate its legitimate uses. Like many tools, the dark web is neutral—its ethical value depends on how it's used. Sensationalism and fear-mongering obscure the complex reality of an internet that is both a force for good and a platform for harm. Only by replacing myth with knowledge can individuals and institutions engage with the digital world in a safe, informed, and responsible manner.

Chapter 2
The Rise of Tor and the Age of Anonymity

In the ever-evolving landscape of the internet, anonymity has emerged as both a shield and a sword—protecting the vulnerable while enabling the dangerous. The second chapter of this journey delves into the powerful tool that made much of the dark web possible: the Tor browser. Often misunderstood and frequently associated solely with illegal activity, Tor is, in reality, a technological innovation rooted in the ideals of privacy, security, and freedom of expression.

Originally developed by the U.S. Naval Research Laboratory in the mid-1990s, Tor—short for "The Onion Router"—was designed to provide anonymous communication for intelligence operations. Its technology, later open-sourced and adopted by a broader global community, gave rise to a unique system of privacy-preserving browsing that became the gateway to the dark web. Today, Tor is not just used by cybercriminals or hackers; it is a lifeline for journalists, whistleblowers, human rights activists, and ordinary individuals seeking protection from surveillance.

This chapter explores how onion routing—Tor's core technology—functions to obscure user identity and protect traffic from tracking and interception. Understanding how this layered system works is key to grasping why the dark web is so difficult to monitor and police.

We will also confront the ongoing debate between anonymous access and illegal activity. Can a tool designed for privacy be blamed for how it's used? What happens when the same technology that shelters dissidents also harbors criminals? These questions don't have simple answers, but they lie at the heart of the digital age's most pressing moral and technological dilemmas.

By tracing the origins and operation of the Tor browser, this chapter sets the stage for understanding not just how people enter the dark web—but why they choose to enter it in the first place.

The Origins of Tor Browser

The origins of the Tor Browser are deeply tied to the evolution of internet privacy, national security, and the growing global demand for anonymous communication in the digital age. To truly understand the dark web and its complexities, one must first understand how Tor—short for "The Onion Router"—was born, what problems it aimed to solve, and how it grew into the gateway to one of the internet's most secretive domains. Far from being the creation of shadowy criminals, Tor was originally designed by government researchers and later embraced by activists, journalists, and everyday users seeking freedom from surveillance.

The concept of onion routing, which underpins the Tor network, was first developed in the mid-1990s by a team at the United States Naval Research Laboratory (NRL). At the time, the U.S. government was increasingly concerned about the ability of foreign powers to monitor its communications across the internet. The early web, though revolutionary, lacked strong privacy protections. Messages and data could be intercepted, traced, and analyzed, leaving intelligence operations, diplomatic correspondence, and military communication vulnerable. The NRL needed a system that could hide not just the content of the message, but also the identity of the sender and recipient.

Their solution was onion routing—a method of encrypting information in multiple layers, much like the layers of an onion. Each layer would be peeled away by a separate relay server in the communication chain, leaving no single server able to trace both the origin and the destination of the data. This method allowed information to pass through the network without revealing the true identity of the user, thus providing a new level of anonymity.

In the early 2000s, this research evolved into what we now know as the Tor Project. With funding from the U.S. Naval Research Laboratory and later support from the Defense Advanced Research Projects Agency (DARPA), the project was designed to not only benefit government operations but also to promote online privacy for civilians. Recognizing the technology's broader potential, the developers released Tor as open-source software in 2002. This decision allowed programmers, researchers, and privacy advocates worldwide to examine, improve, and expand the system. By 2006, the non-profit Tor Project was established, dedicated to maintaining and improving the Tor network.

Initially, Tor's adoption was limited. Few outside of cybersecurity circles knew how to use it, and the public had little awareness of the growing concerns around digital surveillance. That changed dramatically in the 2010s, as governments and corporations increasingly tracked user behavior online. Revelations by whistleblowers like Edward Snowden highlighted the extent of mass surveillance, pushing Tor into the spotlight as a vital tool for protecting privacy and anonymity. Journalists used it to communicate with sources securely, activists in authoritarian regimes relied on it to bypass censorship, and whistleblowers turned to Tor-based platforms like SecureDrop to safely leak sensitive information.

However, the very features that made Tor a sanctuary for free expression also made it attractive to criminals. With anonymity guaranteed, dark web marketplaces like Silk Road emerged, enabling the sale of drugs, counterfeit documents, stolen data, and weapons. While these illicit uses gave Tor a reputation as a haven for crime, the Tor Project consistently emphasized that the technology itself was neutral. It was a tool—how it was used depended on the user. In fact, many of the Tor Project's leaders have spoken openly about their mission to protect free speech and privacy, not to facilitate crime.

The U.S. government's role in Tor's creation has also led to misconceptions. Some believe that Tor was secretly designed as a trap to monitor criminals. In reality, the U.S. initially developed Tor to conceal its own intelligence operations while simultaneously releasing it to the public so that government users could hide in the "crowd" of civilian traffic. By allowing journalists, activists, and ordinary citizens to use Tor, U.S. government communications were less likely to stand out as suspicious.

Today, the Tor Browser remains one of the most widely recognized privacy tools in the world. It operates through a global volunteer network of thousands of relay servers, maintained by individuals and organizations who support online freedom. Its legacy continues to be shaped by the duality of its use: protecting dissidents and journalists on one hand, and being exploited by cybercriminals on the other.

In truth, the origins of Tor are neither purely noble nor purely nefarious. They reflect the paradox of technology itself—created to solve one problem, only to introduce new challenges. What began as a U.S. military project for secure communication has evolved into a symbol of digital anonymity, a double-edged sword that empowers both defenders of human rights and perpetrators of crime. Understanding this history is essential for anyone seeking to make sense of the dark web and the age of anonymity it ushered in.

How Onion Routing Works

When people hear about the dark web and the Tor browser, the question that naturally arises is: how does it actually work? The secret lies in a sophisticated technique called onion routing, a method designed to ensure anonymity and privacy in online communications. Understanding onion routing is crucial because it explains why the dark web is so difficult to monitor, why users can hide their identities, and why both activists and criminals alike rely on this technology.

The term "onion routing" comes from the way the data is protected: it is wrapped in multiple layers of encryption, just like the layers of an onion. Each layer is peeled away by a different relay, or node, in the network, gradually revealing only what is necessary for the message to keep moving forward. At no point does any single relay know both the sender and the receiver, which makes it nearly impossible to trace communication back to its origin.

The process begins when a user opens the Tor Browser to access either the surface web anonymously or hidden services on the dark web. Before the request is sent out, the Tor software randomly selects a path through the Tor network, usually consisting of at least three relays: the entry node, the middle relay, and the exit node. Each node is run by volunteers from around the world, which adds to the network's decentralized nature and makes it harder to compromise.

Here's how the journey unfolds step by step:

1. Encryption Layers Are Built

The user's request—whether it's to visit a news website, send a message, or connect to a .onion service—is encrypted multiple times. Each layer of encryption corresponds to one of the relays in the chosen path. Only the intended relay can peel off its layer to read the routing instructions meant for it. The innermost layer of encryption ensures that only the final destination can read the actual content of the communication.

2. The Entry Node

The request first travels to the entry node. This relay knows the user's IP address but not the final destination. It decrypts the outermost layer of encryption, learns the address of the next relay (the middle node), and passes the remaining encrypted message along. Importantly, the entry node cannot see what the user is accessing, only that they are using Tor.

3. The Middle Relay

Next, the data arrives at the middle relay. This node only knows which relay the message came from (the entry node) and where it's going next (the exit node). It strips away another layer of encryption, forwarding the message without any knowledge of the original sender or the ultimate recipient.

4. The Exit Node

Finally, the request reaches the exit node. This relay removes the last layer of encryption that Tor applied but still cannot identify the original sender. The exit node only sees the content of the communication and its final destination on the internet. If the traffic is unencrypted (such as visiting a regular HTTP site), the exit node could theoretically view the data, which is why security experts recommend accessing only secure websites (HTTPS) through Tor. Once the data leaves the exit node, it proceeds to the destination server just like any other internet request.

5. The Return Path

The response from the destination server follows the reverse path back through the Tor network. Just as with the outgoing request, the response is re-encrypted at each step so that no single relay can reconstruct the full picture of sender, message, and recipient.

This layered system of encryption and routing is what makes Tor so effective at preserving anonymity. Each relay sees only part of the journey, never the whole, ensuring that no single point of compromise can reveal both the user's identity and their online activity.

However, this strength also introduces some weaknesses. Because the data must pass through multiple relays, Tor browsing is significantly slower than normal internet browsing. Users often notice lag or longer loading times. Furthermore, while Tor hides a user's identity, it cannot guarantee complete safety if the user willingly provides personal information, downloads unsafe files, or accesses malicious content.

Another point of vulnerability is the exit node. Since it is the last point before the traffic enters the regular internet, if the destination website does not use encryption (HTTPS), the operator of the exit node could intercept the data. Law enforcement and intelligence agencies sometimes monitor exit nodes to detect illegal activity, though the anonymity of the sender remains intact.

Despite these challenges, onion routing remains one of the most advanced and widely trusted anonymity tools available. Its decentralized structure, combined with volunteer-run relays spread across the globe, makes it extremely resilient to surveillance and censorship. For activists in oppressive regimes, journalists working with sensitive sources, and whistleblowers exposing corruption, onion routing can mean the difference between safety and persecution. At the same time, its protective cloak has made it attractive to cybercriminals running black markets, hacking forums, and other illegal operations on the dark web.

In the end, onion routing is a double-edged sword. It embodies the ideals of privacy and freedom but also enables the darker side of human behavior to thrive. Understanding how it works is key to navigating the ethical dilemmas and security challenges that the dark web presents. Without onion routing, the dark web as we know it today would not exist. With it, the internet has entered an age of anonymity—an era where the line between protection and exploitation grows thinner every day.

Anonymous Access vs Illegal Activity

One of the most hotly debated aspects of the dark web is whether tools like the Tor Browser and onion routing should be viewed primarily as protectors of privacy or as enablers of crime.

The truth, as with most technologies, lies somewhere in the middle. Anonymous access can be a force for good, giving voice to the silenced and protecting those in need of privacy. At the same time, the very features that safeguard legitimate users also create a haven for criminals, black markets, and malicious actors. To truly understand the dark web, it is essential to examine this delicate balance between anonymity as a right and anonymity as a shield for illegal activity.

Anonymity has always been a double-edged sword. On the positive side, it allows people to express themselves freely without fear of retaliation. For individuals living under authoritarian regimes, where censorship is rampant and dissent is dangerous, the ability to access information and communicate anonymously can be lifesaving. Journalists in countries with state-controlled media often use the Tor network to reach international audiences and share uncensored stories. Whistleblowers who expose government corruption or corporate misconduct rely on platforms like SecureDrop—accessible only through Tor—to submit evidence without risking their lives or careers. Similarly, activists working to organize protests or advocate for human rights use anonymous access to avoid surveillance, arrest, or persecution.

Anonymity is also crucial for everyday internet users who simply wish to protect their personal privacy. In a world where companies, governments, and hackers constantly monitor online behavior, many people turn to Tor not because they are hiding crimes but because they want to keep their browsing history, personal communications, and financial information away from prying eyes. For example, a political dissident in a repressive country, a victim of domestic violence seeking help without alerting an abuser, or a citizen researching sensitive health issues may all benefit from the protection Tor provides.

On the other hand, anonymity also creates fertile ground for illegal activity. The dark web is infamous for hosting black markets like Silk Road, AlphaBay, and Hansa, where drugs, counterfeit documents, stolen credit cards, weapons, and even hacking services have been sold. Cybercriminals thrive in these environments, knowing their identities are shielded from authorities. Hackers sell databases of stolen personal information, ransomware developers offer malware for hire, and financial criminals launder money through cryptocurrencies such as Bitcoin or Monero. These marketplaces have generated billions of dollars in illicit trade, creating a global challenge for law enforcement.

One of the most disturbing illegal uses of anonymous access is the distribution of child exploitation material. Despite global efforts to eliminate such content, the dark web provides a hiding place for networks that traffic in these horrific crimes. Similarly, extremist groups and terrorist organizations have been known to use encrypted platforms and the anonymity of Tor to spread propaganda, recruit members, and plan attacks. Although many of these groups are monitored, the cloak of anonymity makes it difficult for intelligence agencies to trace their communications in real time.

A common misconception is that the Tor Project or its developers encourage or condone these activities. In reality, the Tor Project has always been clear that its mission is to protect privacy and free speech. The technology itself is neutral; it is a tool, like a lock or a phone line. Just as a telephone can be used to plan a crime or to call for help, Tor can be used to commit illegal acts or to protect vulnerable individuals. The ethical dilemma lies in the fact that the same feature—anonymity—that shields a political prisoner from a dictatorship can also shield a cybercriminal selling stolen bank credentials.

Law enforcement agencies around the world continue to struggle with this paradox. On one hand, they recognize that anonymity is vital for democracy, free press, and human rights. On the other, they must combat the rise of cybercrime that flourishes in anonymous environments. To address this, agencies like the FBI, Europol, and Interpol have developed advanced digital forensics and undercover operations to infiltrate and dismantle illegal networks on the dark web. Notable cases, such as the shutdowns of Silk Road in 2013 and AlphaBay in 2017, show that anonymity does not guarantee impunity. However, for every marketplace dismantled, another often emerges to take its place.

The debate over anonymous access versus illegal activity also raises important questions about personal responsibility and collective security. Should the average person be denied access to strong privacy tools simply because criminals exploit them? Advocates argue that weakening or banning tools like Tor would harm ordinary citizens far more than it would stop criminals, who would find other ways to hide their activity. Instead, the focus should be on targeting the crimes themselves rather than the technology that enables both good and bad uses.

In essence, anonymous access is not inherently good or bad—it is simply a capability. It empowers the oppressed while simultaneously enabling the lawless. What determines its moral and social impact is not the technology itself but the intentions of those who wield it. The challenge for society lies in maintaining this balance: protecting the right to privacy and free expression without allowing anonymity to become a shield for unchecked criminality.

The rise of Tor and the age of anonymity has forced us to confront these questions more urgently than ever before. As we move deeper into the digital age, this balance between privacy and accountability will remain one of the most critical and controversial issues shaping the future of the internet.

Chapter 3
Entering the Dark Web

For most internet users, the idea of entering the dark web is shrouded in mystery, fear, and curiosity. Unlike the surface web, which is accessible with a simple search and a click, the dark web requires specialized tools, methods, and a certain degree of caution to navigate. This hidden part of the internet is intentionally concealed, designed to protect the anonymity of both visitors and hosts. For some, it is a refuge of free speech and privacy; for others, it is a marketplace of crime and exploitation. The truth lies somewhere in between, and understanding how people access the dark web is the first step in separating myth from reality.

Accessing the dark web is not as simple as opening Google Chrome or Safari. The primary gateway is the Tor Browser, a tool built specifically to allow anonymous access to hidden services, often with URLs ending in .onion. Unlike standard websites, these onion sites are not indexed by search engines and cannot be accessed without the right tools. Additional methods, such as virtual private networks (VPNs), encrypted email services, and secure communication platforms, are often used alongside Tor to enhance privacy and security.

However, gaining access to the dark web is only part of the story. Users must also understand the risks, from encountering scams and malware to stumbling upon illegal content. The dark web is a place where the lines between ethical use and criminal activity blur quickly, making it essential for users to know not only the methods of entry but also the legal and moral boundaries that govern what they do once inside.

In this chapter, we will uncover the tools and methods used to access the dark web, explore the nature of .onion sites and hidden services, and address the delicate balance between privacy rights and the dangers of crossing into illegality.

Tools and Methods Used

Accessing the dark web is not as straightforward as typing a query into Google or clicking a link on your browser. Because the dark web is intentionally hidden from search engines and conventional access points, it requires specialized tools and methods to navigate. These tools are designed to ensure anonymity and security, but they also demand responsibility and caution from the user. Understanding the most common tools and methods used to enter the dark web is essential, whether one's purpose is journalistic research, digital activism, or simple curiosity.

The Tor Browser

The most well-known and widely used tool for accessing the dark web is the Tor Browser, short for The Onion Router. Tor functions by routing internet traffic through a network of volunteer-operated servers, called relays, which encrypt the data in multiple layers. This process makes it extremely difficult for anyone to trace the origin or destination of a user's online activity. Tor is the primary gateway to websites with the ".onion" domain extension, which are not accessible through standard browsers like Chrome, Safari, or Firefox.

Tor is available as a free download and is open-source, meaning that its code is publicly accessible for scrutiny and improvement. Once installed, it looks and functions much like a regular web browser but with enhanced anonymity. Tor also blocks many common tracking technologies, adds security features by default, and allows users to bypass censorship in countries where internet access is restricted.

Virtual Private Networks (VPNs)

While Tor provides anonymity within its network, many users pair it with a Virtual Private Network (VPN) for an added layer of protection. A VPN encrypts internet traffic and routes it through a private server before connecting to Tor. This creates what's known as "Tor over VPN." The advantage of this method is that it prevents Internet Service Providers (ISPs) or local network administrators from detecting that the user is even using Tor. For individuals in highly restrictive countries, a VPN may be essential to avoid suspicion or surveillance when accessing the dark web.

Tails Operating System

Some users go beyond browsers and VPNs by using a dedicated operating system for anonymity, such as Tails (The Amnesic Incognito Live System). Tails is a portable operating system that can be booted from a USB stick or DVD. It is designed to leave no trace on the computer once shut down, ensuring that no activity is recorded locally. Tails comes pre-configured with the Tor Browser and various encryption tools, making it a favorite among journalists, whistleblowers, and activists who require the highest levels of digital security.

Secure Communication Tools

Once on the dark web, secure communication becomes vital. Many users rely on encrypted messaging services like Signal or Ricochet for private conversations. On the dark web itself, some hidden services host encrypted chat rooms where users can interact anonymously. PGP (Pretty Good Privacy) encryption is another common tool, often used to secure emails or confirm the authenticity of messages and transactions. Without such encryption, communications can be intercepted, even within the dark web.

Cryptocurrency Wallets

Since most dark web marketplaces do not accept conventional payment methods, cryptocurrencies are the standard. Bitcoin was once the dominant currency, popularized by the Silk Road marketplace. However, newer cryptocurrencies like Monero and Zcash have gained traction because they offer enhanced privacy features, making transactions harder to trace. Users must set up a secure digital wallet to send and receive these currencies. It is also common to use "mixers" or "tumblers," which shuffle cryptocurrency transactions to obscure their origin and destination.

Dark Web Directories and Forums

Because .onion sites are not indexed by traditional search engines, finding them can be a challenge. To navigate, users often rely on dark web directories, link lists, and forums. Examples include "The Hidden Wiki," which serves as a starting point for many first-time visitors. However, these directories are notoriously unreliable and sometimes dangerous, as many links lead to scams, phishing sites, or illegal content. Experienced users often share trusted addresses privately rather than relying on public directories.

Cybersecurity Practices

Tools alone are not enough; methods and habits play an equally important role in staying safe. Users are advised to disable JavaScript, avoid downloading files, and refrain from sharing personal information under any circumstances. Many rely on strong, randomly generated passwords stored in encrypted password managers. Multi-layered security practices are essential because the dark web is rife with phishing attempts, malware, and deceptive sites designed to exploit careless users.

Challenges and Risks

Even with the best tools, entering the dark web carries risks. Malicious exit nodes may attempt to intercept unencrypted traffic. Marketplaces often harbor scams where sellers disappear after receiving payment. Law enforcement agencies also operate undercover on the dark web, posing as vendors or buyers to track criminal activity. Furthermore, not all security tools are foolproof; a poorly configured VPN, an outdated Tor Browser, or a moment of carelessness can expose a user's identity.

Onion Sites and Hidden Services

The most defining feature of the dark web is its system of .onion sites and hidden services, which together form the unique landscape that distinguishes it from the surface and deep webs. Unlike the familiar websites we access daily, these platforms are designed to conceal the identities of both their hosts and visitors. For many, the very mention of .onion sites conjures images of digital danger, illicit markets, and anonymous criminals. However, the truth is more nuanced: while some of these hidden services host illegal content, others provide critical tools for privacy, journalism, and activism. To truly understand the reality of the dark web, it's essential to explore how .onion sites work, the different roles they play, and the dualities they represent.

What Are .Onion Sites?

At their core, .onion sites are websites that exist within the Tor network and cannot be accessed by regular browsers like Chrome or Safari. They are called ".onion" sites because of their unique domain suffix, which indicates that they are part of the encrypted Tor ecosystem. These sites use complex, randomly generated URLs, such as http://abcd1234xyz.onion, that make them difficult to guess or discover without direct access to the link. This obscurity adds a crucial layer of security and anonymity. Unlike traditional websites that rely on the Domain Name System (DNS), .onion addresses are not registered publicly. Instead, they are generated through cryptographic keys, ensuring that the identity of the site's host is shielded from exposure.

Hidden Services Explained

The term hidden services refers to the infrastructure and services that operate within the Tor network to hide the physical location of the servers themselves. When you visit a surface web site using Tor, your identity may be concealed, but the site's location and server information are still visible. Hidden services take anonymity a step further: not only is the user hidden, but the host of the site remains invisible as well. This is achieved by routing both ends of the connection through multiple relays, preventing either party from discovering the other's true identity or location.

Legitimate Uses of .Onion Sites and Hidden Services

Despite the sensational portrayals often seen in the media, not all .onion sites are dedicated to illegal activity. In fact, many of them serve legitimate, socially valuable purposes.

- **Whistleblowing Platforms:** SecureDrop, an open-source system, allows whistleblowers to share sensitive documents with journalists without fear of being traced. Prominent news organizations such as The New York Times and The Guardian operate .onion versions of their sites for this very purpose.
- **Access to Uncensored Information:** In countries where governments restrict or censor the internet, .onion sites allow citizens to bypass these blocks. The BBC, for example, launched its own Tor mirror site to ensure that people living under repressive regimes could still access unbiased news.
- **Privacy-Focused Services:** Services such as ProtonMail and RiseUp provide .onion access to their encrypted email platforms, ensuring that even users in heavily monitored environments can communicate securely. Similarly, some .onion sites provide secure chat rooms, forums, and file-sharing services.

For many, these hidden services are not a choice but a necessity, offering a lifeline in environments where freedom of speech is severely restricted.

Illicit Uses of .Onion Sites and Hidden Services

Of course, the dark web is also known for harboring illegal activities, and .onion sites play a central role in that.

- **Black Marketplaces:** Perhaps the most infamous use of .onion sites has been in black markets. Sites like Silk Road, AlphaBay, and Hansa facilitated the anonymous trade of drugs, counterfeit documents, hacking services, weapons, and stolen data. Even though many of these markets have been shut down by law enforcement, new ones continue to appear, reflecting the resilience of underground economies.
- **Hacking and Cybercrime Forums:** Many .onion sites serve as forums where hackers exchange stolen data, sell malware, or share techniques for breaching systems. Some even offer "hacking as a service" models for a fee.
- **Child Exploitation Material:** One of the most disturbing aspects of the dark web is its use by criminals to distribute child abuse content. Despite major global crackdowns, the persistence of such sites remains a serious challenge for law enforcement agencies.
- **Fraud and Scams:** The dark web also teems with scam operations. From fake "hitman for hire" services to myths of "red rooms" where users allegedly watch violent acts live for payment, many sites prey on the curiosity and fear of inexperienced visitors. Most of these are scams, but their existence tarnishes the overall reputation of the dark web.

Navigating .Onion Sites Safely

Because .onion sites are not indexed by standard search engines, finding them often involves directories like The Hidden Wiki or recommendations from trusted sources. However, caution is crucial: directories often contain dangerous links that may lead to scams, malware, or illegal content. Experienced users typically rely on verified communities or encrypted networks to share links safely.

To minimize risks, cybersecurity experts recommend:

- Visiting only trusted .onion addresses.
- Avoiding downloads, which may contain malware.
- Using PGP (Pretty Good Privacy) encryption for communication.
- Ensuring that HTTPS is enabled for additional security.
- Keeping Tor and any supporting tools regularly updated.

Law Enforcement and .Onion Sites

Although .onion sites are designed to provide anonymity, they are not invincible. Law enforcement agencies worldwide have grown increasingly skilled at infiltrating and shutting down illegal hidden services. The FBI's takedown of Silk Road in 2013, and later AlphaBay in 2017, demonstrated that operational security mistakes—whether by the operators or their users—can compromise even the most hidden platforms. Agencies use undercover operations, forensic analysis, and international cooperation to combat crimes facilitated through hidden services.

.Onion sites and hidden services represent both the promise and peril of the dark web. They provide invaluable tools for privacy, freedom of expression, and access to uncensored information, yet they also enable some of the most disturbing criminal enterprises in the digital world. Their dual nature reflects the broader paradox of the dark web itself: a place where the pursuit of anonymity can serve both justice and injustice. For those seeking to understand the dark web's reality, recognizing the legitimate and illicit uses of .onion sites is a vital step.

Legal and Ethical Boundaries

The dark web is often described as a lawless frontier, a hidden corner of the internet where rules do not apply. While there is some truth in the idea that it is difficult to regulate, the dark web is not entirely free from oversight or accountability. In fact, legal and ethical boundaries play a crucial role in shaping how individuals, organizations, and governments interact with it. To understand the reality of the dark web, one must separate what is technically possible from what is legally permissible and ethically responsible.

The Legal Landscape

Contrary to popular belief, accessing the dark web is not illegal in most countries. Simply downloading the Tor Browser and exploring .onion sites does not constitute a crime. Tor itself was originally developed with government funding, and its use remains legal as a tool for preserving online anonymity. Journalists, whistleblowers, and citizens in heavily censored countries use Tor daily without breaking any laws.

However, the line is crossed when users engage in illegal activities while on the dark web. These activities include, but are not limited to:

- Purchasing or selling illegal drugs.
- Trading weapons or explosives.
- Distributing child exploitation material.
- Engaging in human trafficking.

- Hiring cybercriminal services, such as hackers for hire.
- Selling or buying stolen personal data, like credit card numbers or medical records.

Law enforcement agencies around the world have successfully infiltrated and dismantled many such operations, proving that anonymity does not mean immunity. Operations against marketplaces like Silk Road and AlphaBay highlight that while it may be difficult to track users, it is not impossible.

It is also important to note that the legal boundaries vary significantly from country to country. In democratic nations, Tor is usually permitted for use, though heavy surveillance may still be applied. In authoritarian regimes, however, simply attempting to access the dark web could raise suspicions of anti-government activity, potentially leading to arrest or interrogation. Thus, legality often depends not only on what one does but also where one lives.

Ethical Considerations

While the law provides a framework for what is permissible, ethics govern what is responsible. Ethical boundaries on the dark web are often more complicated than legal ones, as they touch on personal values, moral beliefs, and the broader impact of one's actions.

For example, consider a journalist using the dark web to communicate securely with a whistleblower. From a legal and ethical standpoint, this can be viewed as a justified use of the platform, ensuring that truth can be revealed without endangering the source. On the other hand, a hacker selling stolen health records to the highest bidder is not only breaking the law but also violating fundamental ethical principles by exploiting others' private lives for personal gain.

The dark web also raises ethical questions about privacy versus accountability. Advocates argue that every individual has a right to digital privacy, and tools like Tor and .onion sites provide a necessary defense against invasive surveillance. Critics counter that anonymity enables criminals to operate unchecked, making it harder to hold them accountable for their actions. Finding the balance between protecting privacy and preventing harm is one of the greatest ethical challenges of the dark web era.

The Gray Areas

Not all activities on the dark web are clearly legal or illegal; some fall into murky gray areas. For instance, in countries where access to uncensored news is blocked, citizens may use .onion mirrors of legitimate news outlets to stay informed. Technically, they may be violating government restrictions, but ethically, they are exercising a fundamental right to information. Similarly, whistleblowers may release classified documents that expose corruption or wrongdoing. While such acts may be illegal under national security laws, many argue they are ethically justified because they serve the public interest.

Cryptocurrencies further complicate these gray areas. While using Bitcoin or Monero for anonymous transactions is legal, regulators worry about how these tools are used to evade taxes, launder money, or fund illicit activities. A user may intend to preserve their privacy in legitimate purchases, but the same system is also used by criminals to obscure illegal trade.

Responsibility of Users

For anyone exploring the dark web, understanding both the legal risks and the ethical implications is essential. Curiosity alone is not a crime, but clicking on the wrong link can expose a user to disturbing or illegal content, even unintentionally. This is why security experts emphasize careful navigation, avoiding unknown sites, and adhering strictly to ethical guidelines. The golden rule is clear: anonymity is a right, but it should never be abused to harm others.

The dark web is neither a utopia of free expression nor a lawless wasteland. It exists in a complex space shaped by both legal frameworks and ethical responsibilities. While its architecture ensures anonymity, the way it is used determines whether it serves as a shield for justice or a cloak for crime. Recognizing the difference between legal access and illegal activity, and balancing privacy rights with ethical considerations, is crucial for anyone seeking to understand or explore this hidden layer of the internet. Ultimately, the dark web reflects humanity itself: capable of profound good, yet always shadowed by the potential for harm.

Chapter 4
Digital Black Markets

For many, the term "dark web" is almost synonymous with digital black markets. These hidden marketplaces, often compared to online versions of Amazon or eBay, have become some of the most notorious elements of the internet's underground world. Accessible only through tools like the Tor Browser, these markets operate beyond the reach of traditional law enforcement and regulators, offering a wide array of goods and services—some legal, but most deeply illegal. From narcotics and counterfeit documents to stolen credit card information and even hacking services, these platforms have transformed the way illicit trade is conducted in the digital age.

The rise of digital black markets began with the launch of Silk Road in 2011, a pioneering dark web marketplace that became infamous for its scale, efficiency, and anonymity. Its creation marked a turning point: the black market was no longer confined to shady street corners or whispered transactions, but instead moved to encrypted online platforms where buyers and sellers could conduct business with relative ease and security. Although law enforcement ultimately shut down Silk Road, its legacy continues to shape the dark web, inspiring countless successors.

At the heart of these markets lies the use of cryptocurrency, which enables anonymous financial transactions that leave little trace for investigators to follow. Bitcoin was the currency of choice in the early days, but newer cryptocurrencies like Monero have since gained popularity for their enhanced privacy features. Combined with the anonymity of Tor, these digital currencies make it extraordinarily difficult to trace transactions back to real-world identities.

In this chapter, we will examine the origins and legacy of Silk Road, the kinds of goods traded on these platforms, and the critical role cryptocurrencies play in fueling the underground economy of the dark web.

The Silk Road Legacy

When the dark web is discussed, no name resonates more powerfully than Silk Road. Launched in 2011, this pioneering online black market changed the way the world thought about illicit trade on the internet. It was more than just a hidden website—it was the blueprint for a new kind of underground economy, one that combined anonymity, technology, and trust in ways the digital world had never seen before. The story of Silk Road is not just about crime but about innovation, ideology, and the enduring impact of one platform on the entire landscape of the dark web.

The Birth of Silk Road

Silk Road was founded by Ross Ulbricht, a 27-year-old with a background in physics and engineering, who adopted the online alias "Dread Pirate Roberts." Ulbricht was not motivated solely by profit; he was heavily influenced by libertarian ideals and the philosophy of the free market. He envisioned a platform where individuals could buy and sell goods without interference from governments or corporations. In his view, Silk Road was not just a marketplace but a demonstration of personal freedom in action.

The platform operated as a hidden service accessible only through the Tor Browser, ensuring that both buyers and sellers remained anonymous. To handle transactions, Silk Road exclusively used Bitcoin, a cryptocurrency that was still relatively unknown at the time. This combination of Tor's anonymity and Bitcoin's pseudonymous transactions created a system that gave users a sense of security while conducting business in a realm largely beyond the reach of law enforcement.

How Silk Road Operated

Silk Road functioned much like mainstream e-commerce platforms such as Amazon or eBay. Sellers could create profiles, list their products, and receive feedback from buyers. Categories ranged from narcotics and counterfeit documents to software tools and more benign products. The platform even had a built-in escrow system, holding buyer payments until the goods were confirmed as delivered, which added a layer of trust and reduced the risk of scams.

What made Silk Road unique was its community-driven model. Buyers and sellers often left detailed reviews and ratings, and there was an emphasis on customer service—even in the illegal trade of drugs. This level of professionalism, combined with the safety of not having to conduct street-level transactions, made Silk Road immensely popular. Within a few years, it grew into a multimillion-dollar enterprise with thousands of listings and tens of thousands of users worldwide.

The Controversy and Criticism

While Ulbricht framed Silk Road as a beacon of liberty and free-market principles, critics and authorities saw it as a dangerous hub for illegal activity. Law enforcement agencies around the globe raised alarms over the platform's role in facilitating the drug trade, enabling the sale of forged passports, and hosting guides on how to commit cybercrimes. Though Ulbricht prohibited the sale of certain items, such as weapons, child exploitation material, and services meant to harm others, the platform still hosted a wide range of contraband.

The debate over Silk Road's morality grew heated. Supporters argued that it reduced street violence by moving drug trade online, where buyers and sellers could interact without physical confrontation. Others contended that it democratized access to substances that many governments unfairly restricted. But critics emphasized the dangers: increased drug availability, potential harm to minors, and the broader challenge it posed to law enforcement and drug control policies.

The Fall of Silk Road

Silk Road's meteoric rise inevitably attracted intense scrutiny from authorities. In 2013, after years of investigation, the FBI managed to shut down the site in a high-profile operation. Ross Ulbricht was arrested in a San Francisco library, caught logged into the administrator's account. Agents seized his laptop, which contained detailed evidence of his role in running the marketplace.

The trial that followed was as controversial as the platform itself. Ulbricht was convicted on charges including money laundering, computer hacking, and conspiracy to traffic narcotics.

He was sentenced to two life terms plus 40 years without the possibility of parole—a sentence many considered excessively harsh. For some, Ulbricht became a martyr for digital freedom, while for others, his punishment was a necessary deterrent.

The Legacy of Silk Road

Although Silk Road was dismantled, its impact did not vanish with it. Instead, it inspired a wave of successor marketplaces, such as Silk Road 2.0, AlphaBay, and Hansa, each building on the foundation it laid. Many of these platforms incorporated stronger security measures to avoid Ulbricht's fate, including encrypted communications and multi-signature escrow systems.

The legacy of Silk Road is twofold. On one hand, it demonstrated how technology could be used to challenge traditional systems of law enforcement and regulation, giving rise to a new era of digital black markets. On the other, it highlighted the dangers of unchecked anonymity, showing how easily illegal trade could flourish under the cloak of privacy.

Even today, years after its takedown, Silk Road continues to be a point of reference in discussions about the dark web. For many, it symbolizes both the promise and peril of digital freedom. Its story is not just about crime but about the power of technology, the complexities of morality, and the never-ending cat-and-mouse game between innovation and regulation.

In many ways, Silk Road was the spark that ignited the dark web economy, and its shadow still looms over every hidden marketplace that followed.

Drugs, Weapons, and Counterfeits

When people imagine the dark web, one of the first things that comes to mind is the trade in illegal goods—particularly drugs, weapons, and counterfeit items. This reputation is not unfounded. Hidden marketplaces on the dark web have become global hubs for these illicit transactions, reshaping the landscape of black-market trade. Unlike traditional street-level crime, which often involves personal risk and violence, the dark web allows individuals to buy and sell illegal products with relative anonymity and reduced physical danger. But this convenience comes with enormous consequences, both for society and for the individuals who participate in these transactions.

The Drug Trade on the Dark Web

The largest and most active category on most dark web marketplaces is narcotics. Drugs ranging from cannabis and ecstasy to heroin, cocaine, and fentanyl are listed in detail, often accompanied by user reviews, seller ratings, and descriptions of quality. The business model mirrors mainstream e-commerce platforms like Amazon, with an emphasis on customer satisfaction and reliable delivery. Many sellers even offer "stealth shipping," concealing the drugs in everyday items or packaging them in a way that avoids detection by customs and postal inspectors.

The availability of such substances online has had a profound effect on the global drug trade. Supporters of dark web markets argue that moving transactions online reduces the violence associated with street-level dealing and allows users to obtain more predictable and higher-quality products, reducing the risk of overdoses from contaminated drugs. Critics, however, highlight that the ease of access increases overall drug consumption and expands the market to include vulnerable groups, including teenagers who may find it easier to purchase illicit substances online than in person.

Law enforcement has struggled to keep pace. While high-profile takedowns such as Silk Road and AlphaBay disrupted the trade, new marketplaces often emerge quickly to take their place, sometimes within weeks. As a result, the online drug trade has become a persistent and resilient phenomenon.

Weapons and Firearms

While the trade in drugs dominates dark web marketplaces, weapons and firearms are another alarming category. Some .onion sites have been known to offer handguns, rifles, and even military-grade weapons. Alongside physical firearms, buyers can also find blueprints for 3D-printed guns, which can be manufactured at home with the right equipment. This poses a particularly serious challenge for authorities because such weapons may bypass traditional registration and tracking systems.

Although weapons sales are less common and often more closely monitored than drug listings, the potential consequences are grave. There have been documented cases of individuals attempting to purchase firearms through the dark web for criminal acts, including terrorism. However, it is worth noting that many of these listings are scams designed to defraud buyers rather than deliver actual weapons. The combination of high demand, limited trust, and heavy surveillance makes weapons trade riskier than narcotics on the dark web.

Counterfeit Goods and Documents

Counterfeit goods represent another major category on the dark web, ranging from fake luxury items to forged passports and driver's licenses. These items are particularly attractive to individuals looking to assume false identities, bypass immigration controls, or commit financial fraud. Forged documents such as birth certificates, university diplomas, and work permits are regularly advertised, often accompanied by guarantees of authenticity and instructions for use.

Financial fraud is also rampant, with counterfeit credit cards, cloned ATM cards, and even "fullz" (complete identity packages containing Social Security numbers, bank account details, and other personal data) sold for cryptocurrency. These identity theft kits allow criminals to open fraudulent bank accounts, apply for loans, or engage in other scams under a stolen identity.

The counterfeit trade also extends to pharmaceuticals. Fake prescription medications, including painkillers, steroids, and psychiatric drugs, are widely available. These counterfeit drugs pose significant health risks because they are often manufactured without quality control, meaning the buyer has no way of knowing what they are ingesting. Cases of poisoning, overdoses, and even death have been linked to counterfeit pharmaceuticals purchased through the dark web.

The Consequences

The availability of drugs, weapons, and counterfeit goods on the dark web has far-reaching implications. Public health suffers as more people experiment with easily accessible drugs. National security is threatened by the potential circulation of untraceable weapons. Economies are destabilized when counterfeit goods undermine legitimate businesses and identity theft drains financial institutions.

Moreover, the anonymity of the dark web emboldens criminal networks that would otherwise struggle to operate in traditional markets. Law enforcement faces significant challenges in tracking transactions, infiltrating networks, and prosecuting offenders. Even when a major marketplace is shut down, the decentralization of the dark web means that replacements quickly emerge, often with improved security measures.

A Marketplace of Trust and Deception

One of the paradoxes of these markets is the reliance on trust in an environment built on secrecy and illegality. Buyers depend on seller ratings, reviews, and escrow systems to ensure that they are not scammed. At the same time, the dark web is rife with fraud. Fake listings, phishing scams, and "exit scams"—in which a marketplace suddenly shuts down and disappears with users' funds—are common. This creates a constant tension between the need for trust and the risk of deception.

The trade in drugs, weapons, and counterfeit goods has cemented the dark web's reputation as a hub for illegal activity. While some argue that online marketplaces reduce physical violence and provide a more controlled environment for illegal trade, the broader consequences are undeniably harmful. The risks of addiction, overdoses, violent crime, and financial fraud cannot be ignored. These illicit markets represent both the ingenuity of digital commerce and the dangers of unchecked anonymity. As long as demand persists and technology enables it, the dark web's trade in contraband will remain a central challenge for societies worldwide.

Cryptocurrency: The Dark Web's Currency

The rise of the dark web and the explosion of digital black markets would never have been possible without the emergence of cryptocurrency. Acting as the financial backbone of the hidden internet economy, cryptocurrencies provide the anonymity, security, and decentralization that traditional banking systems cannot. From the earliest days of Silk Road to today's sophisticated dark web marketplaces, digital currencies have fueled the trade in drugs, weapons, counterfeit goods, and stolen data, all while presenting complex challenges for regulators and law enforcement worldwide.

Why Cryptocurrency Works on the Dark Web

Before cryptocurrency, illicit transactions relied on cash, wire transfers, or other traceable means of payment, all of which posed risks of detection. Cryptocurrencies like Bitcoin introduced a new model: digital, decentralized money not tied to any government or central authority. Transactions occur directly between users, with no bank or intermediary to flag suspicious activity.

This system was ideal for dark web markets, which needed a method of exchange that:

- Protected buyer and seller identities.
- Enabled international transactions without regulation.
- Reduced the risk of law enforcement detection.
- Allowed funds to move quickly and securely.

Although cryptocurrencies are not completely anonymous—Bitcoin transactions are recorded on a public ledger known as the blockchain—they are pseudonymous. This means that transactions are tied to digital wallet addresses rather than real names. When used carefully with tools like Tor, these addresses are difficult to trace back to individuals.

Bitcoin: The Pioneer

When Silk Road launched in 2011, Bitcoin was the currency of choice. At that time, Bitcoin was still in its infancy and largely unknown outside of small online communities. Its early use on Silk Road not only legitimized Bitcoin as a functional currency but also skyrocketed its value and global recognition.

Bitcoin's transparent blockchain, however, soon became a double-edged sword. While users initially believed their transactions were untraceable, law enforcement developed advanced blockchain analysis techniques to track Bitcoin flows. Companies like Chainalysis now assist governments in tracing cryptocurrency used in criminal activities, linking wallet addresses to real-world suspects.

Despite these risks, Bitcoin remains widely used on the dark web due to its accessibility and liquidity. Its popularity ensures that buyers and sellers can easily convert it to and from traditional currency.

The Rise of Privacy Coins

As law enforcement became more skilled at tracing Bitcoin, dark web users began adopting privacy-focused cryptocurrencies that offered stronger anonymity features. Among the most popular are:

- **Monero (XMR):** Designed specifically for privacy, Monero uses advanced cryptographic techniques such as ring signatures, stealth addresses, and confidential transactions to obscure the sender, recipient, and amount of each transaction. This makes Monero far more difficult to track than Bitcoin.

- **Zcash (ZEC):** Another privacy coin, Zcash allows users to choose between transparent and shielded transactions. Its zero-knowledge proofs (zk-SNARKs) enable complete anonymity when selected.
- **Dash and Verge:** Though less popular than Monero, these coins also include privacy-enhancing features, appealing to users seeking alternatives to Bitcoin.

Many dark web marketplaces now prefer or even require payments in Monero, as its built-in privacy protections make it extremely resistant to forensic tracking.

Escrow and Payment Systems

To reduce the risk of scams, most dark web marketplaces operate escrow systems. When a buyer makes a purchase, their cryptocurrency is held in escrow by the platform until the goods are confirmed as delivered. Only then is the payment released to the seller. This adds a layer of trust in an environment where legal enforcement of contracts is impossible.

However, escrow systems have also been exploited. Some marketplaces have conducted exit scams, where administrators abruptly shut down the platform and disappear with all funds held in escrow. This has led to massive losses for both buyers and sellers, reinforcing the volatile nature of the dark web economy.

Cryptocurrency Mixers and Tumblers

To further obscure transactions, many users employ cryptocurrency mixers or tumblers. These services blend multiple transactions together and redistribute the coins, making it difficult to trace the original source. While effective, mixers themselves are often targets for law enforcement, as they are considered money laundering tools in many jurisdictions.

Decentralized mixers and privacy wallets are emerging as alternatives, offering similar services without a central operator that authorities can shut down.

Law Enforcement Challenges

The use of cryptocurrency has posed unprecedented challenges for law enforcement. Unlike traditional banking systems, cryptocurrencies operate outside the control of governments and lack centralized reporting requirements. Even when blockchain analysis tools provide leads, criminals often use multiple layers of wallets, mixers, and privacy coins to cover their tracks.

Nonetheless, law enforcement has made significant progress. The takedowns of Silk Road, AlphaBay, and Hansa included the seizure of millions in cryptocurrency, much of which was later auctioned off by governments. International cooperation has been crucial, with agencies like Europol and the FBI pooling resources to combat cybercrime funded through digital currencies.

The Future of Cryptocurrency on the Dark Web

The role of cryptocurrency in the dark web is likely to grow even more significant as technology evolves. Privacy coins are becoming more sophisticated, blockchain analysis tools more advanced, and the cat-and-mouse game between criminals and authorities more intense. Some experts predict that future dark web markets may adopt decentralized, blockchain-based platforms that eliminate central administrators entirely, making them even harder to shut down.

At the same time, regulators are increasingly focused on cryptocurrency exchanges, forcing them to implement Know Your Customer (KYC) and Anti-Money Laundering (AML) protocols. This makes it harder for criminals to convert cryptocurrency into cash without exposing their identities.

Cryptocurrency is the lifeblood of the dark web economy, providing the anonymity and security that make digital black markets possible. While Bitcoin pioneered this role, privacy coins like Monero now dominate, offering even stronger protections against tracking. Yet the very features that make cryptocurrency attractive to criminals also make it invaluable for activists, journalists, and ordinary users seeking privacy. This dual nature ensures that cryptocurrency will remain central to the dark web's future—for better and for worse.

Chapter 5
The Light Within the Darkness

When most people hear the phrase "dark web," their minds immediately conjure images of drug markets, weapons sales, and other criminal enterprises. While these elements are undeniably present, they represent only one side of the story. The dark web, often painted as a realm of chaos and danger, also serves as a refuge for those seeking safety, truth, and freedom. Beneath the layers of secrecy lies a powerful tool for good—one that provides anonymity not for crime, but for courage.

For whistleblowers, journalists, and human rights activists, the dark web is not a marketplace of vice but a sanctuary where voices can be heard without fear of persecution. In countries where governments silence dissent, censor media, or monitor citizens' every move, platforms built on dark web technology allow the free flow of information. Tools like SecureDrop give whistleblowers the ability to submit evidence of corruption or human rights abuses while protecting their identities. Major news outlets such as The New York Times and The Guardian host .onion versions of their sites to ensure access even in heavily censored regions.

The dark web also functions as a library of banned books, restricted articles, and censored content, granting knowledge to those who would otherwise be denied it. For many, this access to information can mean the difference between ignorance and empowerment.

Perhaps most importantly, the dark web has saved lives. From activists escaping oppressive regimes to citizens finding medical advice in countries where certain treatments are illegal, the dark web provides a digital lifeline where no other options exist.

In this chapter, we will look beyond the shadows of crime to explore the light within the darkness—the platforms, services, and stories that prove the dark web can be a force for truth, justice, and survival.

Whistleblowing and Human Rights Platforms

When we think about the dark web, the dominant narrative is often one of drugs, weapons, and cybercrime. Yet, hidden within this shrouded world are platforms and services that serve as vital lifelines for truth-tellers and defenders of human rights. For whistleblowers, journalists, and activists living under constant surveillance, the dark web offers something rare and precious: the ability to speak freely and securely. Whistleblowing and human rights platforms have become essential tools for exposing corruption, documenting abuses, and preserving the voices of those who would otherwise be silenced.

The Importance of Whistleblowing in the Digital Age

Whistleblowers play a crucial role in democratic societies. By exposing hidden truths—whether they involve government corruption, corporate misconduct, or human rights violations—they hold powerful institutions accountable. However, coming forward with sensitive information is fraught with risk. Whistleblowers may face job loss, public shaming, imprisonment, or even threats to their lives. In countries with authoritarian governments, the dangers are even more severe, with informants often subject to harsh punishment or disappearance.

The dark web provides a solution to this dilemma. Through platforms designed with anonymity in mind, whistleblowers can securely share information without exposing their identity. The most notable of these platforms is SecureDrop, an open-source whistleblowing submission system that operates as a .onion service on the Tor network.

SecureDrop and Journalistic Integrity

Originally developed by the late technologist Aaron Swartz and further advanced by the Freedom of the Press Foundation, SecureDrop has become the gold standard for whistleblower platforms. Dozens of major news outlets—including The New York Times, The Guardian, and The Washington Post—host their own SecureDrop services. These allow whistleblowers to anonymously upload documents, photos, and videos, while also providing a secure way to communicate with journalists.

What makes SecureDrop revolutionary is its emphasis on security at every level. The platform strips metadata from files to prevent accidental exposure, encrypts all submissions, and allows for back-and-forth communication without revealing identities. Whistleblowers are assigned random code names rather than usernames, ensuring even the journalists they communicate with do not know their true identity. This system has empowered countless individuals to expose misconduct while minimizing the risk of retaliation.

The Dark Web and Human Rights Activism

Beyond whistleblowing, the dark web is a powerful ally for human rights organizations and activists, particularly in countries where censorship and surveillance are pervasive. Governments that restrict free speech often monitor internet activity, block websites, and punish those who attempt to speak out. By using the Tor network and hidden services, activists can bypass these restrictions, organize movements, and connect with global audiences.

For example, in regions where independent media outlets are silenced, organizations have launched .onion versions of their websites to ensure access. The BBC and Deutsche Welle both provide Tor mirrors, allowing citizens in censored countries to read unbiased news. Similarly, human rights groups use dark web platforms to collect testimonies, share banned literature, and provide secure communication channels for activists at risk.

Protecting the Vulnerable

The dark web also helps protect vulnerable individuals who seek justice. Victims of domestic abuse, LGBTQ+ communities in hostile environments, and dissidents in oppressive states use anonymous platforms to seek help, share stories, and connect with networks of support. In countries where homosexuality is criminalized, for instance, .onion forums provide safe spaces where members of the community can speak freely without fear of exposure.

Medical support is another area where the dark web has unexpectedly contributed to saving lives. In nations where certain healthcare services are restricted—such as access to contraceptives or safe abortion care—women have used anonymous platforms to seek advice and support from international health organizations. While this remains controversial, it underscores the life-saving potential of anonymity when traditional systems fail.

The Ethical Dimension

The existence of whistleblowing and human rights platforms on the dark web challenges the simplistic notion that anonymity is inherently dangerous. Instead, it shows how anonymity can empower the powerless. However, these platforms must operate with the utmost responsibility. Journalists and organizations running SecureDrop or similar services are tasked with ensuring they do not inadvertently expose their sources. Whistleblowers themselves must also understand that no system is foolproof and must take precautions to protect their identities offline.

It's worth noting that these positive uses of the dark web are often overshadowed by the sensationalist focus on illegal markets. Yet, for many around the world, these hidden services are not optional curiosities—they are essential tools of survival and justice. The dark web becomes, in these cases, not a den of crime but a sanctuary of truth.

Law Enforcement and the Balance of Power

Law enforcement agencies face a difficult balance when dealing with anonymity tools. On the one hand, they must combat the very real crimes taking place on the dark web. On the other, they cannot afford to undermine technologies that protect whistleblowers and activists. Increasingly, there are calls for governments to recognize and even support platforms that promote accountability and transparency while continuing to target criminal misuse of the same technologies.

Whistleblowing and human rights platforms represent the brighter side of the dark web, offering anonymity not for the purpose of exploitation but for protection and empowerment. They demonstrate how the very same tools that facilitate illegal trade can also safeguard democracy, freedom, and human dignity. In a world where surveillance is increasing and freedom of speech is under constant threat, these platforms provide a vital reminder: the dark web is not only a marketplace for crime, but also a stage for courage.

Banned Books and Journalistic Access

When people think of the dark web, they often focus on its dangers and criminal enterprises. Yet, beneath the layers of secrecy lies a different reality—one in which knowledge and information, often suppressed or outright banned, find a safe refuge. The dark web has become an underground library of sorts, giving access to banned books, censored content, and platforms for journalism in countries where free expression is stifled. For countless individuals, these hidden resources are not luxuries but necessities—gateways to truth in societies built on control and misinformation.

The Power of Banned Books

Throughout history, books have been among the first casualties of censorship. Authoritarian regimes and oppressive governments have long feared the power of the written word to inspire resistance, question authority, and spread ideas that challenge the status quo. From George Orwell's 1984 and Salman Rushdie's The Satanic Verses to political memoirs and religious texts, many works have been banned at different times for their content.

On the surface web, censorship is often effective because traditional publishers and online platforms are subject to government regulation. But on the dark web, banned literature continues to thrive. Digital copies of controversial books circulate freely through .onion libraries and hidden archives, accessible to anyone with the right tools. These repositories act as virtual sanctuaries for knowledge, preserving works that authorities seek to erase from public consciousness.

For citizens living under censorship, access to these texts can be transformative. They provide not only intellectual enrichment but also empowerment, showing readers that they are not alone in questioning authority. In societies where propaganda dominates education and media, banned books often represent the first step toward independent thought.

Hidden Libraries on the Dark Web

One of the most notable uses of the dark web is the creation of hidden digital libraries. These archives contain vast collections of books, academic papers, and political essays, often including works banned or restricted in certain countries. Examples include libraries that specialize in preserving religious texts outlawed in specific regions or collections of historical documents that governments prefer to keep buried.

These libraries are not operated for profit; most are run by volunteers and activists committed to the principle that information should be free and accessible. They rely on the anonymity of the Tor network to protect both their operators and their readers. For many users, these hidden collections are their only means of accessing uncensored knowledge without fear of surveillance or punishment.

Journalistic Access and Free Press

Just as books face censorship, so too does journalism. In many parts of the world, independent journalism is under siege. Reporters are silenced, websites are blocked, and citizens are fed a steady diet of state-approved propaganda. The dark web, however, provides a powerful workaround.

Major international news organizations such as The New York Times, The Guardian, BBC, and ProPublica have established .onion versions of their websites. These hidden sites allow readers in heavily censored countries to bypass government blocks and access independent reporting. In countries where authorities control the flow of information, these dark web platforms provide a crucial window to the outside world.

For journalists themselves, the dark web is equally vital. It provides secure channels for communicating with sources, sharing documents, and publishing stories that would otherwise be impossible to distribute safely. Platforms like SecureDrop allow reporters to receive sensitive information anonymously, enabling investigative journalism that might expose corruption, human rights abuses, or crimes committed by powerful individuals.

When Access Saves Lives

The significance of these resources goes beyond intellectual curiosity. For some, accessing banned books and uncensored journalism on the dark web is a matter of survival. Consider activists in regions where speaking against the government is punishable by imprisonment or worse. For them, access to censored information can mean the difference between blindly following propaganda and finding the courage to resist.

Similarly, in countries where health information is censored—such as guidance on sexual health, reproductive rights, or LGBTQ+ issues—the dark web provides vital resources that save lives. Hidden sites host medical literature and practical advice that is otherwise restricted, giving individuals the knowledge they need to make informed decisions about their health and safety.

The Ethical Debate

The use of the dark web for banned books and journalism is not without controversy. Governments often label these activities as subversive or illegal, accusing participants of undermining national security. Critics argue that the dark web can also be used to spread dangerous misinformation or extremist propaganda. The challenge lies in distinguishing between the preservation of truth and the dissemination of harmful content.

Despite these concerns, the ethical case for providing access to censored information is strong. Knowledge, after all, is a fundamental human right, and denying it creates environments where injustice and oppression flourish unchecked. The dark web's role in preserving banned books and supporting independent journalism highlights its potential as a force for empowerment rather than exploitation.

While the dark web is often associated with crime and secrecy, its role in preserving access to banned books and independent journalism cannot be overstated. For millions living under censorship, these hidden libraries and news platforms represent hope, freedom, and truth. They remind us that information, once shared, is almost impossible to silence completely. In the tunnels of the dark web, ideas outlawed in one place find safe passage to others, ensuring that even in the darkest corners of human control, light still finds a way to shine.

When the Dark Web Saves Lives

The dark web is often portrayed in mainstream media as a breeding ground for crime, fear, and danger. While these portrayals are not without merit, they overlook an equally compelling narrative—the ways in which the dark web has, quite literally, saved lives. For activists, whistleblowers, marginalized groups, and individuals in oppressive environments, the anonymity and security provided by dark web platforms have offered protection, freedom, and even survival. Far from being only a digital underworld of crime, the dark web has also proven to be a sanctuary of safety and hope.

Protecting Whistleblowers and Dissidents

Whistleblowers who expose government corruption, corporate malfeasance, or human rights abuses often face devastating consequences. Many risk imprisonment, exile, or death for speaking the truth. The dark web has given these brave individuals a secure outlet to share their evidence without revealing their identities. Platforms like SecureDrop and GlobaLeaks provide safe channels for uploading documents, photos, and testimony, which can then reach trusted journalists.

Consider a whistleblower in a country where criticizing the government is a crime. Without the anonymity of the dark web, exposing corruption would be suicidal. With these platforms, they can provide critical information to global media outlets while remaining hidden. These acts of courage, facilitated by anonymity, have exposed crimes that might otherwise have remained buried forever.

Saving Lives Through Access to Information

For citizens in heavily censored nations, access to the truth can mean the difference between oppression and freedom. State-controlled media often paints a false picture of reality, leaving people with no way to question what they are told. By accessing uncensored journalism through .onion mirrors of organizations like the BBC or ProPublica, individuals gain knowledge that empowers them to resist manipulation.

Beyond political truth, the dark web also provides life-saving access to medical information. In countries where topics such as reproductive health, LGBTQ+ support, or mental health are censored, hidden websites offer vital resources. Women in restrictive regimes have used the dark web to access advice on safe abortions when no legal options were available. LGBTQ+ individuals in hostile societies have found support networks, counseling resources, and even safe meeting points through dark web forums. In these cases, the information accessed is not merely enlightening—it is life-preserving.

Escaping Surveillance and Oppression

For many living under authoritarian governments, every online action is monitored. Speaking freely, attending protests, or even visiting the wrong website can trigger suspicion. The Tor network allows citizens to bypass government firewalls and surveillance, granting them safe spaces to organize resistance, communicate securely, and share uncensored information.

During periods of political unrest, activists have relied on dark web communication tools to coordinate demonstrations, avoid crackdowns, and share real-time updates with the world. Without these hidden channels, many of these movements would have been swiftly crushed, their voices silenced before they could reach beyond their borders.

Support for Victims of Abuse and Exploitation

The dark web has also played a role in supporting victims of domestic violence, human trafficking, and exploitation. Survivors can use anonymous forums and encrypted chatrooms to seek help, share their stories, and connect with organizations willing to provide assistance. In cases where abusers monitor internet activity or control physical access to communication devices, the anonymity of the dark web provides a rare lifeline for escape.

For victims of trafficking, some hidden services have enabled them to reach out discreetly to humanitarian organizations, offering a chance for rescue that would be impossible through conventional, monitored channels. While the same technology is unfortunately exploited by traffickers themselves, it also provides opportunities for intervention and survival for victims brave enough to reach out.

The Ethical Balance

It is important to acknowledge that the very tools that save lives can also be exploited by criminals. This paradox creates an ethical dilemma for governments, tech companies, and human rights advocates. Should anonymity be curtailed to reduce crime, even if doing so risks exposing whistleblowers and activists to persecution? Or should the right to privacy be protected at all costs, even if it means criminals also benefit?

Many argue that removing the protections of anonymity would do more harm than good, silencing those who need it most while failing to stop determined criminals, who would simply find other means to hide. The lives saved through access to hidden platforms and secure communication make a strong case for preserving anonymity, despite its risks.

Real-World Examples

Over the years, numerous cases have illustrated how the dark web saves lives:

- Arab Spring Activists: During uprisings across the Middle East, many used Tor and dark web platforms to share uncensored reports and organize protests without detection.
- Medical Access: In countries with strict bans on certain health services, underground medical communities have provided life-saving information and even directed individuals to safe providers.
- Journalistic Protection: Reporters in countries like Russia and China have used dark web platforms to safely receive tips and publish reports that would otherwise be suppressed.

The dark web is not a monolithic space of crime and danger. It is a complex ecosystem where light and darkness coexist. For every illicit marketplace, there is a platform offering truth, safety, and hope to those who need it most. When viewed through this lens, the dark web is not merely a hidden world of vice but also a digital sanctuary where lives are protected, voices are amplified, and freedom finds a way to survive.

Chapter 6
The Psychology of the Hidden User

The dark web is more than just a technological phenomenon; it is also a deeply human one. Behind every anonymous username, encrypted message, and hidden transaction lies a person with motivations, fears, and desires. To understand the reality of the dark web, it is not enough to explore its marketplaces, platforms, or technologies—we must also examine the psychology of the hidden user.

Why do people turn to the dark web in the first place? For some, it is necessity: whistleblowers protecting their identities, activists escaping censorship, or citizens searching for medical advice in countries where such information is restricted. For others, it is curiosity, a desire to explore the forbidden corners of the internet and uncover truths hidden from the surface web. And then there are those driven by darker motivations—criminals seeking profit, thrill-seekers indulging in taboo activities, or individuals looking for anonymity to commit acts they would never attempt in the open.

Central to this psychological shift is what researchers call the anonymity effect—the way people behave differently when they believe their identity is hidden. Freed from accountability, users often feel emboldened to act in ways they would avoid under scrutiny, whether that means speaking truth to power or engaging in risky and illegal behaviors.

The dark web also taps into powerful emotional currents: the fear of being watched, the desire for absolute freedom, and the temptation of forbidden desires. These forces shape not only individual behavior but also the culture of the dark web itself.

In this chapter, we will dive into the minds of hidden users, exploring who they are, why they come, and how anonymity transforms both their actions and their sense of self.

Who Uses the Dark Web—and Why?

The dark web is often described as a mysterious place populated exclusively by criminals, hackers, and other malicious actors. While it is true that illegal activities occur there, this narrow portrayal ignores the wide range of people who use the dark web and the diverse motivations behind their presence. From whistleblowers and journalists to everyday citizens and organized crime groups, the dark web attracts individuals for reasons that span from noble to nefarious. Understanding **who uses the dark web—and why—**is essential to separating myth from reality.

Whistleblowers and Journalists

One of the most significant groups using the dark web includes whistleblowers and journalists. In societies where exposing corruption or misconduct can lead to imprisonment or death, anonymity is not a luxury—it is a necessity. Platforms like **SecureDrop** and **GlobaLeaks** enable whistleblowers to safely leak documents and evidence to trusted media organizations without fear of reprisal. Many leading news outlets, including *The New York Times* and *The Guardian,* maintain .onion portals specifically to receive anonymous submissions. For these users, the dark web is not about crime but about truth and accountability.

Activists and Human Rights Defenders

In authoritarian regimes, activists rely on the dark web to communicate, organize, and access uncensored information. When governments block social media or shut down internet access, hidden services provide secure channels for coordination. During the Arab Spring uprisings, for example, activists turned to anonymity networks to share updates and avoid surveillance. Today, the dark web continues to serve as a critical lifeline for dissidents and marginalized groups seeking freedom of speech, political reform, and basic human rights.

Everyday Privacy Seekers

Not all dark web users are involved in high-stakes political or journalistic activity. Many are ordinary people concerned about their privacy in a world where surveillance has become routine. From avoiding corporate data mining to protecting personal searches from prying eyes, these users leverage Tor and other dark web tools for peace of mind. They may visit dark web email providers, private chatrooms, or .onion versions of mainstream websites to escape constant tracking. In essence, they are using the dark web not to commit crimes but to reclaim their right to privacy.

Researchers and Academics

Cybersecurity experts, law enforcement professionals, and academics also frequent the dark web for research purposes. By monitoring illicit forums and marketplaces, they gain insights into criminal networks, emerging cyber threats, and the tools hackers are selling or developing. Universities and think tanks sometimes sponsor research projects to better understand the behaviors and economics of dark web markets. For these users, the dark web is both a laboratory and a window into hidden aspects of the digital world.

Criminal Enterprises

Of course, the dark web does host a significant criminal presence. Organized crime groups, individual hackers, and fraudsters use it as a platform to sell illegal goods and services. Narcotics remain one of the most popular categories, with dark web markets functioning like anonymous versions of eBay. Other criminals trade in weapons, counterfeit documents, malware, stolen financial data, and hacking-for-hire services. The anonymity of cryptocurrencies such as Bitcoin and Monero fuels these transactions, making it difficult for law enforcement to track.

For these users, the appeal of the dark web lies not only in anonymity but also in convenience. Buying drugs, stolen credit cards, or even forged passports online removes the risks of face-to-face transactions and allows access to a global customer base. The dark web provides criminals with both security and efficiency, reshaping the traditional underground economy.

Curiosity-Driven Users

Another group often overlooked is the curious. These are individuals who venture into the dark web out of interest or fascination rather than necessity. They may have heard stories about "red rooms" or hidden markets and want to see for themselves what lies beyond the surface web. While curiosity-driven users may not intend to engage in illegal activity, their lack of caution can expose them to scams, malware, or disturbing content. For some, curiosity evolves into deeper involvement, while others retreat quickly after realizing the risks.

Victims Seeking Help

Perhaps one of the most unexpected categories of dark web users includes victims of abuse, discrimination, or exploitation. For example, individuals in LGBTQ+ communities living under oppressive laws may turn to hidden forums for support. Victims of domestic violence might use the dark web to connect with advocacy groups without their abusers discovering their online activity. In countries where health information is restricted, people seek advice and guidance from medical forums hosted on the dark web. For these vulnerable individuals, anonymity can literally save lives.

The Complex Picture

What emerges from this landscape is a complex picture: the dark web is not solely a haven for criminals, nor is it purely a sanctuary for truth-seekers. It is both. The motivations for using the dark web are as diverse as the people themselves. Some use it to protect their freedoms, others to exploit the freedoms of anonymity for selfish or destructive ends. Between them lie those who are simply curious or in need of protection that the surface web cannot provide.

The question of **who uses the dark web—and why—**cannot be answered with a simple stereotype. It is a digital crossroads where courage meets corruption, where victims find lifelines, and where criminals conduct business under the same cloak of anonymity that protects whistleblowers and activists. To understand the reality of the dark web, we must recognize this diversity. It is not a space defined by a single narrative but by the coexistence of many, each shaped by the universal human desire for safety, freedom, and, sometimes, power.

Fear, Freedom, and Forbidden Desires

The dark web is often described as a realm cloaked in shadows, a place where secrecy and anonymity create a world vastly different from the surface internet. To understand why people are drawn to it, we must look beyond the technical layers of encryption and onion routing and examine the emotional and psychological dimensions. The dark web thrives on three interconnected forces: fear, freedom, and forbidden desires. These elements shape not only why individuals use the dark web but also how they behave once inside it.

The Power of Fear

Fear is perhaps the most primal force that drives people to the dark web. In authoritarian regimes, fear of government surveillance, censorship, or punishment compels citizens, journalists, and activists to seek safe spaces where they can speak freely. The knowledge that every online action is monitored, every post scrutinized, and every message potentially intercepted creates an environment where silence becomes survival.

For these individuals, the dark web offers not just anonymity but also a rare sense of security. They use hidden platforms to bypass firewalls, access blocked information, and communicate with others without the looming threat of imprisonment or retaliation. Fear of exposure drives them to adopt Tor, encrypted messaging, and other tools that allow them to remain invisible in a digital world built on constant observation.

But fear is not limited to oppressive governments. Even in democratic societies, citizens increasingly worry about corporate surveillance, identity theft, and data exploitation. The fear of losing control over personal information pushes many to the dark web, where privacy feels more attainable. Here, fear transforms into caution, shaping careful browsing habits and reliance on security tools to maintain safety.

The Allure of Freedom

If fear drives people into the dark web, freedom keeps them there. The ability to browse, communicate, and transact without oversight is liberating. On the surface web, digital footprints are constantly tracked by corporations, governments, and advertisers. In contrast, the dark web promises a world where identities are masked, activities are hidden, and users can reclaim a sense of autonomy.

For whistleblowers and activists, this freedom means being able to share the truth without risking their lives. For ordinary citizens, it can mean exploring ideas, books, or communities that may be stigmatized or censored in their societies. The dark web is a rare digital frontier where freedom of expression is not just a principle but a practice.

However, freedom in this context is a double-edged sword. While it empowers the oppressed and marginalized, it also provides cover for criminals, extremists, and those who thrive on lawlessness.

This paradox is central to the dark web's identity: the same tools that protect journalists also shield drug traffickers; the same networks that give voice to activists also amplify the reach of cybercriminals.

The Temptation of Forbidden Desires

Perhaps the most controversial dimension of dark web psychology is the pursuit of forbidden desires. The anonymity of the dark web emboldens individuals to seek out what they would never dare pursue on the surface. Some of these desires are harmless curiosities—such as exploring banned literature or uncensored political opinions—while others cross into morally and legally dangerous territory.

The concept of "forbidden fruit" plays heavily into this dynamic. The very fact that certain content is hidden or taboo makes it more alluring. Whether it is access to illicit substances, counterfeit goods, or underground forums, the thrill of breaking boundaries entices users who might otherwise never engage in such activities. The dark web becomes a digital playground for exploring curiosity without immediate social or legal consequences—though the risks remain real.

This aspect of forbidden desire also highlights a darker truth: anonymity can strip away the inhibitions that guide behavior in public spaces. Psychologists refer to this as the online disinhibition effect—the tendency for people to behave more boldly, aggressively, or recklessly online when shielded from accountability. In the dark web, where accountability is almost nonexistent, these tendencies are magnified.

The Interplay of Fear, Freedom, and Desire

What makes the dark web unique is not the existence of fear, freedom, or forbidden desire alone, but how they interact. Fear pushes people to seek protection; freedom reassures them that protection is possible; and forbidden desires tempt them to explore what lies beyond the boundaries of conventional morality. Together, these forces create an ecosystem that is both empowering and dangerous, noble and corrupt.

For some, this triad serves as a catalyst for courage. Activists in censored nations use their fear as fuel, harness freedom to share truth, and overcome the forbidden barrier of speaking against authority. For others, it becomes a slippery slope, where the thrill of forbidden desires eclipses ethical boundaries and leads to criminal behavior.

The psychology of the dark web cannot be understood without acknowledging the roles of fear, freedom, and forbidden desires. These elements are the invisible threads that weave the culture of the hidden internet. For some, the dark web is a sanctuary where fear is calmed and freedom flourishes. For others, it is a stage where forbidden desires take center stage, leading them into moral or legal jeopardy. Ultimately, the dark web mirrors the complexities of human nature itself—where the quest for safety and freedom collides with the temptation to explore the forbidden.

Chapter 7
Law Enforcement in the Shadows

For all its promises of anonymity and secrecy, the dark web is not beyond the reach of the law. While many believe it to be an impenetrable fortress where criminals operate with impunity, law enforcement agencies across the globe have proven otherwise. The battle between those who exploit the dark web and the authorities who pursue them has evolved into a high-stakes digital chess game—one fought in the shadows of encryption, anonymity, and cyber intelligence.

From the early days of Silk Road to the takedown of AlphaBay, law enforcement has repeatedly demonstrated that the so-called "untraceable" can, in fact, be traced. Yet the methods used are far from conventional. Instead of relying on traditional policing, agencies employ advanced digital forensics, undercover cyber stings, and international cooperation to infiltrate hidden networks and identify their operators. Mistakes made by criminals—whether technical errors, trust in the wrong person, or lapses in operational security—often become the keys to their downfall.

But this cat-and-mouse game is far from over. As law enforcement develops new strategies, dark web operators respond with more sophisticated technologies and tighter security measures. The struggle is constant, with neither side able to claim absolute victory.

In this chapter, we will uncover how agencies monitor what many consider "untraceable," revisit the dramatic stories behind the falls of Silk Road and AlphaBay, and explore the intricate world of cyber stings and digital forensics. Together, these stories reveal a powerful truth: the dark web may offer anonymity, but it is not a guarantee of safety from the long arm of the law.

How Agencies Monitor the Untraceable

The dark web was built on the promise of anonymity, using layers of encryption and hidden services to shield both users and hosts from prying eyes. For many, it feels like an invisible realm, immune to surveillance and law enforcement. Yet, despite these protective measures, agencies across the globe have developed sophisticated strategies to monitor, infiltrate, and dismantle criminal operations hidden within it. The process is neither simple nor guaranteed, but the belief that the dark web is "untraceable" is, in reality, a dangerous myth.

The Challenge of Anonymity

The very foundation of the dark web—the Tor network and onion routing—makes monitoring an extraordinary challenge. Unlike the surface web, where IP addresses and traffic patterns are relatively easy to track, dark web communication passes through multiple relays, with each one peeling away a layer of encryption.

This ensures that no single node knows both the sender and the receiver. For law enforcement, this means traditional surveillance tools often fail to reveal identities or server locations.

Despite this, agencies have learned that anonymity is not absolute. Human error, technical flaws, and operational slip-ups often provide the weak points needed to pierce the veil of secrecy. Criminals may log in without using proper precautions, leave digital footprints on the surface web, or inadvertently reveal personal details in communications. Monitoring the dark web is less about breaking encryption and more about exploiting these vulnerabilities.

Open Source Intelligence (OSINT)

A significant portion of dark web monitoring relies on Open Source Intelligence (OSINT). Investigators collect and analyze data from public forums, directories, and chatrooms to map criminal networks and identify potential suspects. Even within the dark web, where users often feel invisible, discussions, user handles, and transaction histories can leave behind patterns. Linking activity across different platforms—sometimes to surface web accounts—can gradually unmask individuals.

For instance, a dark web vendor might use the same pseudonym on a mainstream social media platform or inadvertently reveal personal information while discussing sales. Such mistakes provide entry points for investigators to begin building profiles.

Undercover Operations

Another critical tactic is undercover infiltration. Law enforcement officers create fake identities and interact directly with dark web communities, posing as buyers, sellers, or service providers. By gaining trust within these circles, they collect intelligence, identify key players, and sometimes even take control of marketplaces.

One famous example was the takedown of the Hansa marketplace in 2017, when Dutch law enforcement secretly seized the platform's servers and continued running it for a month. During that time, investigators collected data on thousands of transactions and users, leading to numerous arrests worldwide. This operation showed that even the most careful dark web criminals could be tricked by clever infiltration.

Technical Surveillance and Digital Forensics

While onion routing is nearly impossible to crack directly, law enforcement agencies employ advanced digital forensic tools to monitor activities indirectly. For example, they may track cryptocurrency transactions, analyze malware distributed through the dark web, or identify weaknesses in server configurations.

Blockchain analysis has become a powerful weapon in the fight against dark web crime. Though Bitcoin and other cryptocurrencies are touted as anonymous, their public ledgers allow investigators to trace transactions with the help of specialized companies like Chainalysis. By following the flow of funds and identifying chokepoints—such as exchanges where cryptocurrency is converted to cash—authorities can connect digital wallets to real-world identities.

Additionally, some agencies exploit vulnerabilities in the Tor Browser itself. On rare occasions, law enforcement has deployed custom malware to de-anonymize users by forcing their browsers to leak identifying information, such as IP addresses. These highly targeted operations, while controversial, have led to the capture of dark web administrators and child exploitation site operators.

International Cooperation

No single country can tackle dark web crime alone. The hidden nature of the dark web means that criminals, servers, and buyers are often scattered across multiple nations. As a result, international cooperation is essential. Agencies such as Europol, Interpol, and the FBI frequently work together, pooling resources and intelligence. Joint operations allow investigators to track suspects across borders, seize servers hosted in different jurisdictions, and coordinate arrests on a global scale.

The takedown of AlphaBay in 2017, for example, involved collaboration between U.S., European, and Thai authorities. The operation was a clear demonstration that even international criminal enterprises could be dismantled through coordinated effort.

The Role of Human Error

Despite all the technology and strategy, one of law enforcement's greatest assets remains human error. Many dark web users overestimate the security of their environment and fail to take basic precautions. Using personal email addresses, reusing usernames, logging in without a VPN, or boasting about illegal activities on the surface web often provides the evidence needed to unmask them.

Ross Ulbricht, the founder of Silk Road, was ultimately caught not because Tor was broken but because of operational mistakes. He used his real name in early online posts promoting Silk Road and logged into administrator accounts in public spaces, where agents could seize his laptop while it was still unlocked.

The dark web was designed to be a sanctuary of anonymity, but law enforcement agencies have proven that it is far from invincible. Through a combination of OSINT, undercover operations, digital forensics, blockchain analysis, and international cooperation, they have turned the supposedly "untraceable" into a battlefield where mistakes can mean exposure. The cat-and-mouse struggle between dark web criminals and law enforcement continues, with each side constantly evolving. One truth remains clear: the promise of total invisibility is an illusion.

The Fall of Silk Road & AlphaBay

The dark web's rise to infamy is inseparable from two of its most notorious marketplaces: Silk Road and AlphaBay. These platforms transformed the way illicit goods were bought and sold, creating multi-million-dollar underground economies hidden behind layers of encryption and cryptocurrency. But while they were hailed by their users as untraceable sanctuaries of anonymity, their eventual downfall proved a sobering truth: even in the shadows, law enforcement has a long reach. The stories of Silk Road and AlphaBay are not just tales of digital black markets—they are case studies in how ingenuity, arrogance, and human error collide with relentless investigation.

The Rise of Silk Road

Launched in 2011 by Ross Ulbricht, known by his pseudonym Dread Pirate Roberts, Silk Road quickly became the dark web's most famous marketplace. Ulbricht envisioned a libertarian free market beyond the control of governments and corporations, where individuals could buy and sell as they pleased. Built as a Tor hidden service and fueled by Bitcoin transactions, Silk Road allowed users to purchase narcotics, counterfeit documents, hacking tools, and other illicit goods with a level of anonymity previously unimaginable.

By 2013, Silk Road was generating over $1 billion in total sales and had become the poster child of the dark web. Its customer-service model, complete with seller ratings, escrow systems, and dispute resolution, made it function much like Amazon—but for illegal products.

The Fall of Silk Road

Despite the promise of anonymity, Ulbricht made critical operational mistakes. Early forum posts promoting Silk Road were traced back to his real name, and undercover agents infiltrated the site as buyers and sellers. In October 2013, after a lengthy investigation, the FBI arrested Ulbricht in a San Francisco library. Agents seized his laptop while it was open and logged in, providing access to evidence tying him directly to the site's operations.

The takedown of Silk Road was a landmark moment. Ulbricht was convicted of money laundering, computer hacking, and conspiracy to traffic narcotics, receiving a sentence of two life terms plus 40 years without parole. While some hailed him as a visionary, others saw him as a reckless criminal. His arrest sent shockwaves through the dark web, but it did not end the phenomenon—if anything, it inspired successors.

The Rise of AlphaBay

Among the successors was AlphaBay, launched in 2014 by Alexandre Cazes, a Canadian national living in Thailand. Unlike Silk Road, which was run largely by one individual, AlphaBay was a more sophisticated operation with a team of administrators and developers. Within three years, it had become the largest dark web marketplace in history, hosting over 350,000 listings, including drugs, weapons, malware, and stolen data.

AlphaBay's scale dwarfed Silk Road. Estimates suggest it facilitated between $600 million and $800 million in transactions, making it the dominant hub of dark web commerce. To enhance anonymity, AlphaBay not only accepted Bitcoin but also adopted Monero, a privacy-focused cryptocurrency harder to trace. Its sheer size and technical sophistication made many users believe it was invulnerable.

The Fall of AlphaBay

Yet, AlphaBay's success also made it a prime target. International law enforcement agencies, including the FBI, DEA, Europol, and the Royal Thai Police, launched a coordinated investigation. The operation was highly secretive and relied on both digital forensics and good old-fashioned detective work.

Cazes, the site's founder, made the fatal mistake of reusing email addresses from his personal life for administrative tasks tied to AlphaBay. Investigators also traced cryptocurrency flows connected to his financial accounts. In July 2017, Cazes was arrested at his home in Bangkok. Authorities seized his laptop, which was still logged in as AlphaBay's administrator, along with millions of dollars in assets, luxury cars, and properties.

Tragically, only a week after his arrest, Cazes was found dead in his jail cell, reportedly by suicide. AlphaBay was officially shut down, and the operation was hailed as one of the most significant victories in the fight against dark web crime.

The Impact of the Takedowns

The collapse of Silk Road and AlphaBay sent clear messages to the dark web community: anonymity is not absolute, and law enforcement is both patient and persistent. These takedowns disrupted the flow of illegal goods and instilled fear among vendors and buyers alike. However, the dark web's resilience was also evident. New marketplaces emerged to fill the void, including Dream Market and Wall Street Market, though many were short-lived or plagued by scams.

Law enforcement also used the opportunity to gather intelligence. During the AlphaBay takedown, agencies secretly monitored users migrating to other platforms, identifying key players and tracking cryptocurrency movements. The operation highlighted the importance of international cooperation and the blending of cyber forensics with traditional investigative methods.

The stories of Silk Road and AlphaBay illustrate both the ingenuity of dark web marketplaces and the inevitability of their downfall. Their rise demonstrated the potential of anonymity and cryptocurrency to fuel digital black markets; their fall revealed the cracks in even the most carefully constructed systems. In the end, it was not a failure of technology but human error—careless posts, reused emails, and operational slip-ups—that exposed their leaders. For law enforcement, these victories proved that even in the deepest shadows, there are ways to shine a light.

Cyber Stings and Digital Forensics

When people imagine the dark web, they often see it as a digital fortress—sealed by layers of encryption, protected by anonymity, and beyond the reach of law enforcement. Yet history has proven otherwise. The takedowns of marketplaces like Silk Road and AlphaBay demonstrate that the dark web is not impenetrable. Behind these victories lies a combination of two powerful tools: cyber stings and digital forensics. These methods have become the cornerstone of modern policing in cyberspace, allowing authorities to outwit criminals who believe themselves untouchable.

The Concept of Cyber Stings

A cyber sting is essentially an undercover operation conducted in the digital world. Much like traditional stings, where officers pose as criminals or buyers to catch offenders, cyber stings involve law enforcement officers creating fake identities on the dark web. These identities might appear to be drug buyers, hackers for hire, or even administrators of dark web forums. By blending into these hidden communities, agents gain valuable intelligence and sometimes even control over illicit operations.

One of the most famous examples occurred in 2017, when Dutch authorities secretly seized control of Hansa Market, one of the dark web's largest marketplaces. Instead of immediately shutting it down, investigators ran the site for weeks, gathering data on thousands of buyers and sellers. During that time, AlphaBay, the largest dark web market, was simultaneously taken offline, pushing many of its users to Hansa. Unbeknownst to them, they were walking straight into a trap. This cyber sting operation led to countless arrests and dismantled criminal networks across the globe.

The Role of Digital Forensics

While cyber stings focus on infiltration, digital forensics involves gathering, analyzing, and interpreting digital evidence. On the dark web, this includes everything from tracking cryptocurrency transactions to recovering deleted files and identifying malware. Forensic specialists are often the unsung heroes of these investigations, combing through encrypted hard drives, dissecting code, and reconstructing user activities.

One of the most powerful forensic tools in law enforcement's arsenal is blockchain analysis. Although cryptocurrencies like Bitcoin were once believed to be anonymous, investigators quickly learned that the blockchain—the public ledger recording every transaction—could be analyzed to trace funds. By following the digital trail and identifying choke points where criminals convert cryptocurrency into fiat money through exchanges, agencies have successfully linked transactions to real-world identities.

Exploiting Human Error

Despite the sophistication of dark web technologies, the biggest vulnerability often lies not in the systems but in the people using them. Digital forensics experts regularly exploit human errors to unmask criminals. This may include:

- Reused usernames across the surface web and dark web.
- Personal information accidentally shared in communications.
- Poorly configured servers leaking metadata.
- Criminals accessing accounts without using a VPN or Tor properly.

Ross Ulbricht, the creator of Silk Road, famously fell victim to such mistakes, using his real name in early posts and leaving his laptop logged in when arrested. Similarly, Alexandre Cazes of AlphaBay was exposed through reused email addresses tied to personal accounts. These small lapses, combined with forensic analysis, proved critical in their downfall.

Malware and Tracking Tools

Law enforcement has also developed custom tools to deanonymize users. In some cases, agencies deploy malware through dark web sites that secretly collects information from visitors' devices, such as IP addresses. A notable example occurred during the FBI's Operation Pacifier in 2015, which targeted a child exploitation site. Investigators took control of the site and used a Network Investigative Technique (NIT) to identify thousands of users worldwide. Although controversial, these techniques highlight the evolving nature of digital stings.

International Cooperation

Cyber stings and digital forensics rarely succeed without international collaboration. Criminals, servers, and buyers are often scattered across the globe, making jurisdiction a significant challenge. Organizations like Europol and Interpol coordinate multinational investigations, pooling forensic expertise and intelligence. The AlphaBay and Hansa operations are prime examples of this teamwork, with agencies from the United States, Europe, and Asia working together to execute simultaneous takedowns.

Ethical and Legal Challenges

The use of cyber stings and digital forensics raises significant ethical and legal questions. Deploying malware or secretly operating dark web marketplaces risks entrapping users or exposing innocent individuals to surveillance. Critics argue that some tactics blur the line between lawful investigation and unlawful intrusion. Courts worldwide continue to grapple with these dilemmas, balancing the urgent need to combat dark web crime with the obligation to uphold civil liberties and due process.

The Ongoing Cat-and-Mouse Game

Despite law enforcement's successes, criminals on the dark web continue to adapt. New marketplaces emerge with enhanced security measures, such as multi-signature escrow systems and the adoption of privacy-focused cryptocurrencies like Monero. In response, law enforcement agencies refine their forensic techniques and expand their undercover operations. This ongoing cat-and-mouse game ensures that the battle between law enforcement and dark web criminals remains dynamic, with no end in sight.

Cyber stings and digital forensics have proven that the dark web is not the untouchable fortress many believe it to be. Through undercover infiltration, blockchain analysis, forensic expertise, and international collaboration, law enforcement has dismantled some of the largest criminal enterprises in the digital underground. Yet, as quickly as one market falls, another rises, each more resilient and cautious than the last. The dark web may promise anonymity, but as history shows, those who believe they are truly untraceable often find themselves ensnared by the very shadows they trust.

Chapter 8
Terrorism and Extremism Online

The dark web, while often associated with black markets and cybercrime, has also become a powerful tool in the hands of terrorists and extremist groups. Beyond encrypted communications and hidden transactions, it provides these organizations with a platform to spread propaganda, recruit followers, and coordinate operations far from the eyes of mainstream surveillance. For governments and security agencies, this evolution has created one of the most complex and urgent challenges of the digital age.

Unlike traditional media, where extremist messages can be monitored and removed, the dark web offers anonymity and resilience. Terrorist groups exploit hidden forums, encrypted chatrooms, and .onion sites to distribute propaganda videos, manifestos, and training manuals that are difficult to censor. These platforms also allow extremists to radicalize individuals, often targeting vulnerable people through carefully crafted messages that appeal to identity, belonging, or revenge.

Recruitment on the dark web has moved beyond geographical boundaries, enabling extremist ideologies to spread across continents with unprecedented speed. From providing instructions on bomb-making to encouraging lone-wolf attacks, these hidden networks have become incubators for violent action.

At the same time, the rise of online extremism has forced governments and counterterrorism agencies to adapt. Law enforcement and intelligence services now employ advanced cyber surveillance, digital forensics, and undercover operations to infiltrate extremist communities and disrupt their networks. The battle is not only about shutting down sites but also about countering the narratives that fuel radicalization.

In this chapter, we will explore how extremist groups use the dark web to distribute propaganda, recruit and radicalize individuals, and how counterterrorism agencies are fighting back in this invisible war. The stakes are high, for in this hidden corner of the internet, the consequences of inaction can be devastating.

Propaganda Distribution

The dark web has given extremist and terrorist organizations a powerful new weapon: the ability to spread propaganda globally with minimal risk of detection or censorship. In the past, extremist groups relied on physical pamphlets, underground meetings, or illicit radio broadcasts to spread their ideologies. Today, with the anonymity provided by Tor and encrypted platforms, they can distribute their messages instantly to audiences across continents. Propaganda distribution on the dark web has become one of the most pressing security challenges of the digital age, shaping not only how extremist ideologies spread but also how they recruit, radicalize, and sustain their networks.

Why the Dark Web Appeals to Extremists

The surface web and mainstream social media platforms like Facebook, Twitter (X), and YouTube remain primary outlets for extremist propaganda. However, these platforms are under increasing pressure from governments and advocacy groups to monitor and remove extremist content quickly. As a result, many organizations and individuals who promote extremist ideologies migrate to the dark web, where content is harder to track and almost impossible to take down once published.

The anonymity of the dark web allows extremist groups to:

- Avoid surveillance by intelligence and law enforcement agencies.
- Host videos, manifestos, and training manuals without the risk of immediate removal.
- Communicate securely with sympathizers and operatives worldwide.
- Create archives of material that remain accessible despite takedowns on the surface web.

For groups whose very survival depends on secrecy and reach, the dark web provides the ideal ecosystem.

Types of Propaganda on the Dark Web

Extremist propaganda takes many forms, and the dark web serves as a repository for nearly all of them.

1. Videos and Speeches:

High-production videos are often distributed to glorify terrorist leaders, celebrate attacks, or promote ideological justifications.

These videos frequently include graphic imagery intended to shock, intimidate, and inspire followers.

2. Manifestos and Literature:

Extremist writings—such as religious interpretations, political manifestos, or guides to violent action—are often stored in dark web libraries. For instance, digital archives contain translations of radical texts that are banned in many countries.

3. Training Manuals:

The dark web is rife with downloadable documents and PDFs offering instructions on bomb-making, cyber warfare, or guerrilla tactics. These materials are often shared in encrypted forums to minimize exposure to outsiders.

4. Magazines and Newsletters:

Some extremist groups, such as ISIS in its prime, produced regular online magazines like Dabiq and Rumiyah. While often circulated initially through the surface web, archived versions remain available on the dark web long after removal elsewhere.

5. Propaganda Games and Media:

In some cases, extremist groups have experimented with interactive content, such as simple video games or posters designed to appeal to younger audiences and normalize violent ideologies.

Methods of Distribution

Propaganda on the dark web is distributed using a mix of open and closed channels.

- **Onion Websites:** Extremist groups create dedicated .onion sites hosting archives of propaganda material. These sites are often promoted within hidden forums and constantly change addresses to avoid takedowns.

- **Encrypted Forums and Chatrooms:** Invitation-only forums allow vetted members to share propaganda while also fostering discussions around ideology and tactics.
- **Peer-to-Peer Networks:** Some groups use decentralized file-sharing systems that make removing material virtually impossible.
- **Link Sharing on the Surface Web:** Occasionally, links to dark web propaganda sites are briefly posted on the surface web or mainstream platforms to attract new users before being quickly deleted.

Psychological Impact of Dark Web Propaganda

The effectiveness of extremist propaganda lies not only in its content but in its psychological delivery. By offering anonymity, the dark web allows individuals to explore extremist materials without fear of being monitored, creating a sense of safety that encourages deeper engagement.

For sympathizers already inclined toward extremist ideas, these materials provide validation and a sense of belonging. For undecided individuals, propaganda often presents emotionally charged narratives designed to evoke anger, injustice, or pride. The combination of powerful imagery, religious or ideological justifications, and promises of community creates a potent mix for radicalization.

Challenges for Law Enforcement

Combating propaganda distribution on the dark web poses unique challenges:

- **Persistence of Content:** Once uploaded, files can be copied and rehosted endlessly, making complete removal nearly impossible.
- **Anonymity of Users:** The Tor network conceals both uploaders and consumers, complicating identification.
- **Volume and Diversity:** The sheer amount of propaganda makes it difficult to monitor every channel.
- **Cross-Border Jurisdiction:** Servers hosting extremist content may be in countries with little interest in cooperating with international law enforcement.

Countermeasures and Responses

Despite these challenges, governments and security agencies employ multiple strategies to combat extremist propaganda.

- **Undercover Infiltration:** Intelligence officers join extremist forums to monitor discussions, collect data, and identify key propagandists.
- **Cyber Takedowns:** Coordinated efforts sometimes succeed in shutting down .onion sites hosting propaganda, though they often reappear elsewhere.
- **Counter-Narratives:** Some organizations produce content aimed at debunking extremist ideologies, offering alternative perspectives and undermining the appeal of propaganda.

- **Blockchain and Digital Forensics:** When propaganda involves fundraising through cryptocurrency, investigators trace the flow of funds to disrupt financial support.

The distribution of propaganda on the dark web is one of the most potent tools in the arsenal of modern extremist groups. By exploiting anonymity and encryption, they have created networks of influence that transcend borders and evade censorship. While law enforcement continues to adapt, the persistence and adaptability of extremist propaganda underscore the difficulty of erasing dangerous ideas once they take root. Ultimately, the battle is not only technological but ideological, requiring both strong security measures and compelling counter-narratives to diminish the dark web's role as a breeding ground for extremism.

Recruiting and Radicalizing

One of the most troubling uses of the dark web by extremist and terrorist groups is the recruitment and radicalization of new members. While surface web platforms like social media remain important entry points for propaganda, the dark web offers a more private, controlled, and anonymous environment where radicalization can take root and deepen. Here, away from the scrutiny of governments and mainstream platforms, extremist groups can groom individuals, build loyalty, and prepare them for real-world action.

Why the Dark Web Is Attractive for Recruitment

The dark web offers several advantages that make it a prime environment for recruiting and radicalizing individuals:

1. **Anonymity and Security:** Potential recruits can explore extremist content without fear of immediate exposure. This anonymity reduces hesitation and encourages individuals to engage with material they might avoid on the open web.
2. **Exclusive Appeal:** Hidden forums and invite-only communities create a sense of belonging and importance. Being given access can make recruits feel "chosen" or part of an elite circle.
3. **Control of Narrative:** Unlike mainstream platforms that may moderate content, extremist groups on the dark web can distribute unfiltered messages, indoctrinating recruits without interruption.
4. **Safe Communication Channels:** Through encrypted chatrooms, .onion forums, and peer-to-peer messaging systems, recruiters can have direct, private conversations with potential members.

The Stages of Radicalization Online

Recruitment and radicalization on the dark web often follow a deliberate process:

1. **Exposure:** Individuals may first encounter extremist content on the surface web—perhaps a video clip, a social media post, or a piece of propaganda. From there, they are directed to dark web sites for deeper involvement.
2. **Engagement:** On hidden forums, recruits begin interacting with community members. Discussions, videos, and literature provide ideological frameworks that explain perceived injustices and outline solutions through extremist action.

3. **Commitment:** Through constant reinforcement, recruits adopt extremist beliefs as part of their identity. They may participate in online rituals, pledge loyalty, or become more active in spreading propaganda.
4. **Action:** In some cases, radicalization culminates in real-world activities, ranging from fundraising and cyberattacks to participating in violent acts or providing material support to extremist organizations.

Methods of Recruitment

Extremist recruiters on the dark web employ a variety of tactics to attract and retain new members:

- **Personalized Outreach:** Recruiters often use encrypted one-on-one chats to develop personal relationships with potential members, exploiting feelings of isolation, anger, or identity crisis.
- **Community Building:** Forums and chatrooms foster a sense of brotherhood or shared mission, making recruits feel part of something greater than themselves.
- **Ideological Indoctrination:** Recruits are supplied with articles, books, manifestos, and videos that reinforce the extremist worldview. Content is often framed around themes of victimhood, heroism, and divine or moral duty.
- **Gamification of Radicalization:** Some groups use digital rewards, badges, or status rankings within forums to incentivize active participation and loyalty.
- **Encouragement of Lone-Wolf Attacks:** Recruiters may urge individuals to act independently, reducing the risk of

organizational exposure. Step-by-step guides for small-scale attacks are often provided.

Target Demographics

While anyone can become a target, extremist recruiters often focus on specific groups more vulnerable to their messaging:

- **Disenfranchised Youth:** Young people struggling with identity, purpose, or belonging are frequent targets, as they may be more impressionable and eager to join a cause.
- **Political Dissidents:** Those already disillusioned with their governments or societies may be more receptive to extremist ideologies.
- **Marginalized Communities:** Individuals facing social or economic exclusion may find validation and empowerment in extremist narratives.
- **Curious Visitors:** Some recruits begin as curious explorers of the dark web, only to be gradually drawn into extremist content through exposure and engagement.

Case Examples

Groups like ISIS became notorious for their recruitment strategies. While much of their early success came from surface web propaganda, hidden sites and encrypted forums allowed them to continue grooming recruits even after mainstream platforms cracked down on their content. Recruits were often given step-by-step instructions: from pledging allegiance to the group to carrying out acts of violence in their own countries.

Right-wing extremist groups have also taken advantage of the dark web. Forums dedicated to white supremacist ideologies and anti-government rhetoric provide echo chambers where individuals are radicalized without external challenge.

Challenges for Law Enforcement

Recruitment and radicalization on the dark web are particularly difficult to counter:

- **Secrecy:** Encrypted communications make it hard for investigators to identify and monitor conversations.
- **Global Reach:** Recruiters and recruits may be in different countries, complicating jurisdiction and response.
- **Psychological Manipulation:** Radicalization is often gradual and deeply personal, making it harder to disrupt once it takes root.
- **Self-Radicalization:** Some individuals consume propaganda independently, becoming radicalized without direct recruiter contact, making early detection nearly impossible.

Countermeasures

Despite the challenges, governments and organizations have adopted strategies to combat recruitment on the dark web:

- **Undercover Infiltration:** Agents pose as recruits to gather intelligence and identify recruiters.
- **Disruption of Forums:** Authorities target and dismantle extremist forums, disrupting networks before they can grow.
- **Counter-Narratives:** Programs create alternative content that challenges extremist ideologies and offers healthier avenues for identity and belonging.

- **Community Engagement:** Social and educational initiatives aim to address the underlying grievances that make individuals vulnerable to radicalization.

Recruitment and radicalization on the dark web illustrate the dangerous synergy of technology and ideology. By offering anonymity, exclusivity, and community, the dark web provides extremists with powerful tools to attract and indoctrinate new members. Combating this threat requires not only technological intervention but also a deep understanding of the psychological and social forces that drive individuals into the arms of extremism. The battle against radicalization online is as much about winning hearts and minds as it is about shutting down forums and intercepting messages.

Counterterrorism Tactics on the Web

The spread of terrorism and extremism online—particularly through the dark web—has created one of the most complex challenges for modern security forces. Unlike traditional battlefields, the digital landscape is decentralized, hidden, and global, enabling extremist groups to recruit, communicate, and plan without geographic boundaries. In response, governments and intelligence agencies have had to evolve rapidly, developing sophisticated counterterrorism tactics on the web to disrupt propaganda, recruitment, and operational planning.

Intelligence Gathering and Surveillance

The first line of defense in counterterrorism efforts is intelligence gathering. Agencies rely on a combination of open-source intelligence (OSINT), which involves collecting publicly available data, and dark web monitoring, which targets extremist forums, encrypted chatrooms, and hidden sites.

Specialized algorithms are used to detect keywords, suspicious behavior, and encrypted traffic patterns that may indicate extremist activity. Artificial intelligence and machine learning models are increasingly employed to analyze massive amounts of data, identifying potential threats before they manifest into attacks.

In addition, agencies use human intelligence (HUMINT)—infiltrating extremist communities with undercover operatives or informants who build trust and provide inside information. This blending of digital surveillance with traditional intelligence gathering has proven critical in anticipating and disrupting terrorist plots.

Infiltration and Undercover Operations

One of the most effective tactics against online terrorism involves direct infiltration. Just as law enforcement agents pose as drug buyers in dark web markets, counterterrorism units create fake identities to join extremist groups online. They participate in discussions, observe recruitment strategies, and collect intelligence on key figures.

For example, after ISIS began using encrypted channels for recruitment, intelligence agencies around the world deployed undercover officers to penetrate these networks. In some cases, agents even posed as potential recruits to gain deeper access to leadership circles. This approach not only exposes recruitment pipelines but also allows agencies to map out networks of sympathizers and supporters.

Cyber Takedowns and Site Disruptions

Disrupting extremist infrastructure is another key tactic. Governments have launched coordinated cyber takedowns of extremist websites and forums, seizing servers or rendering sites inaccessible. The goal is twofold: cut off communication channels and demonstrate that anonymity is not absolute.

However, takedowns often face challenges. Extremist sites frequently reappear under new domain names or migrate to decentralized platforms that are harder to dismantle. To counter this, agencies have shifted toward continuous disruption rather than one-time takedowns, aiming to destabilize extremist communications over time rather than eliminating them completely.

Tracking Financial Flows

Terrorist groups require funding to operate, and the dark web often plays a role in their financial activities. Counterterrorism agencies use blockchain analysis to trace cryptocurrency transactions linked to extremist groups. While privacy-focused coins like Monero pose challenges, forensic tools have become increasingly advanced at identifying suspicious patterns and connecting wallet addresses to real-world individuals.

Cutting off financial resources has proven to be one of the most effective ways to weaken extremist organizations. By tracking donations, illicit trade, and cryptocurrency laundering schemes, authorities can disrupt the flow of money that sustains online propaganda and recruitment efforts.

Counter-Narratives and Online Campaigns

While surveillance and infiltration are important, counterterrorism experts acknowledge that fighting extremist ideologies also requires counter-narratives. These are online campaigns designed to challenge extremist propaganda and offer alternative viewpoints.

Non-governmental organizations, community leaders, and even former extremists are often involved in producing counter-narrative content. Videos, articles, and testimonials are crafted to expose the lies of extremist ideology, humanize its victims, and provide positive outlets for identity and belonging. By undermining the emotional and psychological appeal of extremist messages, counter-narratives aim to reduce the pool of vulnerable recruits.

For instance, several programs in Europe have worked with former extremists to create content warning young people about the dangers of radicalization. Similarly, Muslim scholars and clerics have used dark web platforms to provide theological rebuttals to radical interpretations of Islam used by groups like ISIS and Al-Qaeda.

International Cooperation

Because terrorism is a global threat, no single country can address it alone. International cooperation is vital in counterterrorism efforts. Organizations such as Europol, Interpol, and the United Nations Counter-Terrorism Committee facilitate intelligence sharing and joint operations.

The takedown of AlphaBay and Hansa markets, while largely targeting illegal trade, also disrupted extremist fundraising channels. These operations demonstrated the power of multinational cooperation, combining cyber forensics, undercover stings, and simultaneous arrests across different continents.

Ethical and Legal Challenges

Counterterrorism tactics on the web are not without controversy. Critics argue that aggressive surveillance programs risk violating privacy rights and could target innocent individuals. Deploying malware or monitoring encrypted conversations raises questions about legality and civil liberties. Striking the balance between security and individual freedoms remains one of the most difficult aspects of online counterterrorism.

Additionally, the reliance on undercover operations raises concerns about entrapment, where individuals might be pushed into actions they would not have otherwise taken. Courts and policymakers continue to grapple with how far agencies should go in infiltrating and disrupting extremist networks without undermining fundamental democratic values.

Counterterrorism on the dark web is a battle fought on multiple fronts—through intelligence gathering, undercover infiltration, digital forensics, cyber takedowns, financial disruption, and counter-narratives. While extremist groups exploit anonymity and encryption to spread their messages, law enforcement and intelligence agencies have proven resourceful and adaptive in their efforts to combat them.

Chapter 9
Identity Theft and Data Leaks

Few crimes on the dark web are as widespread—or as personally devastating—as identity theft and data leaks. In today's hyperconnected world, personal information has become one of the most valuable commodities on the underground market. From stolen passwords and hacked credit cards to entire digital identities, the dark web thrives on trading what many of us take for granted: our privacy.

The black markets of the dark web, often referred to as "password dumps" or "credit card bazaars," are filled with massive databases of breached information. Hackers collect this data through phishing schemes, malware, ransomware attacks, or breaches of major corporations. Once obtained, it is packaged, advertised, and sold to the highest bidder, often in bulk, for surprisingly little money. A single purchase can contain thousands—or even millions—of usernames, passwords, and credit card details.

For criminals, these data troves are goldmines. They can use stolen identities to open fraudulent bank accounts, drain savings, apply for loans, commit tax fraud, or make purchases using hijacked credit cards. Beyond immediate financial harm, victims often face years of stress as they attempt to restore their credit and secure their personal information.

The trade extends beyond raw data. Entire "digital lives" are sold on the dark web—complete packages of personal information including social security numbers, medical records, addresses, and even browsing histories. These full identity kits allow criminals to impersonate victims in nearly every aspect of their online and offline lives.

Adding to the threat is the rise of Ransomware-as-a-Service (RaaS) and Exploits-as-a-Service, where even inexperienced hackers can rent tools to launch attacks. This democratization of cybercrime has fueled an alarming increase in breaches and leaks.

In this chapter, we will explore the dark web's role in identity theft, how stolen data is packaged and sold, and the devastating impact it has on individuals and society at large.

Password Dumps and Credit Card Bazaars

When most people imagine the dark web, they think of drugs, weapons, and extremist content. Yet one of the most common and profitable trades in this hidden ecosystem is far more personal: the buying and selling of stolen credentials and financial information. From massive password dumps to sprawling credit card bazaars, the dark web has become a thriving marketplace for identity theft. These transactions not only fuel billions of dollars in fraud each year but also leave countless victims struggling to regain control over their digital lives.

The Rise of Password Dumps

A password dump is a collection of stolen usernames and passwords, usually gathered from data breaches of major corporations, government databases, or popular online services. Hackers infiltrate servers, steal the data, and then post or sell it on the dark web. Some dumps are leaked for free as a show of power or to build reputation within hacking communities, while others are sold for profit.

These dumps often contain millions—or even billions—of records. For example, the infamous "Collection #1" leak in 2019 exposed over 770 million email addresses and 21 million unique passwords. Such massive compilations are prized by criminals because they provide endless opportunities for "credential stuffing"—a technique where stolen username-password pairs are tested across multiple websites, exploiting the fact that many users reuse passwords.

Password dumps are especially dangerous because they often include not only login credentials but also personal details like names, phone numbers, and addresses. With this information, criminals can break into email accounts, social media profiles, online banking systems, and more, wreaking havoc on victims' lives.

Credit Card Bazaars: The Dark Web's Black Markets

Alongside password dumps, credit card bazaars form another cornerstone of the dark web economy. These marketplaces, often modeled after legitimate e-commerce sites, sell stolen payment card information obtained through hacks, skimming devices, phishing attacks, or malware installed on point-of-sale systems.

Vendors typically offer packages containing card numbers, expiration dates, CVV codes, and sometimes the cardholder's full name and billing address. Prices vary depending on the type and quality of the data. A standard U.S. credit card might sell for as little as $5, while premium cards with high limits or additional personal information ("fullz") can fetch up to $100 or more. Bulk deals are common, with entire databases of stolen cards sold to professional fraud rings.

In addition to selling raw card data, some bazaars provide automated tools that help criminals test cards in real time to determine whether they are still active. Others bundle their products with tutorials, customer support, and even replacement policies if the stolen cards no longer work—mirroring the professionalism of legitimate online businesses.

How Criminals Use Stolen Credentials

Stolen passwords and payment information are highly versatile. Criminals can:

- Commit financial fraud by making unauthorized purchases or transferring money.
- Steal identities to open new accounts, apply for loans, or commit tax fraud.
- Hijack email or social media accounts to scam victims' friends and families.
- Launch ransomware attacks using compromised login details to infiltrate corporate systems.
- Sell access to others, creating layers of exploitation as data circulates through multiple hands.

Some stolen credentials are used immediately, while others are stored and resold repeatedly, prolonging the risk for victims.

The Ecosystem Behind the Markets

Password dumps and credit card bazaars don't exist in isolation—they are supported by a broader ecosystem of cybercrime services:

- **Malware Developers:** Create viruses, keyloggers, and phishing kits to harvest credentials.
- **Data Brokers:** Act as intermediaries who compile, organize, and sell stolen data.
- **Mixers and Tumblers:** Obscure the flow of cryptocurrency payments used in transactions.
- **Hosting Services:** Provide bulletproof servers that resist takedown attempts from law enforcement.

This network ensures that even if one marketplace is shut down, others quickly rise to take its place, keeping the flow of stolen data constant.

The Human Cost

While the trade in stolen credentials may seem abstract, the consequences for victims are devastating. Identity theft can take months—or even years—to resolve. Victims may face drained bank accounts, ruined credit scores, denial of loans, and relentless harassment from debt collectors. Beyond the financial losses, many experience profound psychological stress, anxiety, and a lasting sense of vulnerability.

For businesses, breaches that lead to password dumps and credit card sales can result in massive financial penalties, loss of customer trust, and class-action lawsuits. A single breach can cost millions in damages, not to mention the long-term reputational harm.

Law Enforcement Efforts

Governments and agencies worldwide have launched numerous operations to combat these markets. The U.S. Secret Service, Europol, and Interpol regularly target large-scale fraud rings, while cybersecurity firms monitor dark web marketplaces for stolen credentials. However, the sheer volume of breaches and the global nature of the dark web make complete eradication impossible.

Some agencies have had success infiltrating bazaars, posing as buyers or sellers to gather intelligence and identify key players. Others collaborate with cryptocurrency tracing companies to follow money trails and disrupt financial flows. Still, the adaptability of these markets ensures that they remain a persistent threat.

Password dumps and credit card bazaars are among the dark web's most profitable and pervasive trades. They illustrate how anonymity and encryption have fueled a thriving underground economy built on stolen identities. For victims, the impact extends far beyond financial loss, often leading to lasting emotional and psychological scars. Despite aggressive efforts by law enforcement, the demand for stolen credentials ensures that these markets continue to flourish, proving that in the digital age, our identities are among the most valuable—and vulnerable—currencies of all.

Selling Your Digital Life

In today's interconnected world, our personal information is more valuable than most of us realize. Every click, purchase, message, and online registration creates a digital footprint—a collection of data that tells the story of who we are, what we like, and how we live. On the dark web, this digital footprint is not just data; it's currency. Entire "digital lives" are packaged, sold, and resold in underground markets, providing criminals with the keys to impersonate victims, commit fraud, and exploit identities in ways most people never imagine.

What Does a "Digital Life" Consist Of?

A digital life kit is a complete package of an individual's personal and financial information. Unlike basic stolen credentials such as a single username or credit card number, these kits are comprehensive. They may include:

- Full name, date of birth, and address.
- Social Security or national identification numbers.
- Bank account and credit card details.
- Login credentials for email, social media, and online shopping accounts.
- Medical records, insurance information, and even biometric data.
- Browsing history and location data collected through compromised devices.

In the underground markets, these bundles are often referred to as "fullz" (slang for "full information"). With a fullz package, a criminal can essentially step into the digital shoes of a victim, accessing financial accounts, applying for loans, filing false tax returns, or even creating fraudulent passports and IDs.

How Criminals Obtain Digital Lives

The data that fuels this trade comes from a variety of sources:

1. **Data Breaches:** Massive corporate breaches are the leading source of stolen personal information. Hackers exploit vulnerabilities in servers, extracting millions of records at once.
2. **Phishing Attacks:** Fake emails, messages, or websites trick users into handing over login details or sensitive personal data.
3. **Malware and Spyware:** Keyloggers, trojans, and spyware silently collect passwords, browsing histories, and even webcam feeds from infected devices.
4. **Social Engineering:** Criminals exploit human psychology, manipulating people into revealing confidential information.
5. **Dark Web Brokers:** Some criminals specialize in compiling data from multiple breaches, creating detailed identity kits for resale.

The Economics of Selling Digital Lives

On the dark web, the sale of digital lives is big business. Prices vary depending on the quality and depth of the information. A single email password might sell for just $2, but a complete identity package with bank details and verified financial accounts can fetch hundreds of dollars.

Some marketplaces operate like traditional e-commerce platforms, with sellers offering ratings, customer support, and guarantees. Buyers are assured that the data is "fresh" (not yet flagged by banks or authorities), and some vendors even replace non-working credentials. The professionalism of these markets often shocks newcomers, but it reflects the billions of dollars flowing through the underground identity theft economy.

How Stolen Digital Lives Are Used

The purchase of a digital life gives criminals broad power to exploit victims. Some of the most common uses include:

- **Financial Fraud:** Accessing bank accounts, draining funds, or making unauthorized purchases.
- **Loan and Credit Scams:** Using personal details to apply for loans, credit cards, or even mortgages.
- **Tax Fraud:** Filing false tax returns to steal refunds.
- Medical Identity Theft: Using insurance information to obtain treatments or prescription drugs.
- **Synthetic Identities:** Combining real and fake data to create entirely new, untraceable identities used in long-term fraud schemes.
- **Blackmail and Extortion:** Threatening to release sensitive personal data or private browsing histories unless victims pay a ransom.

The Human and Social Impact

The sale of digital lives is not a victimless crime. For individuals, identity theft can lead to financial devastation, ruined credit scores, and years of emotional stress as they try to repair the damage. Victims often feel violated, knowing that strangers have access to the most intimate details of their lives.

For society at large, the trade fuels a cycle of distrust and insecurity. Businesses lose billions annually responding to fraud, while governments are forced to invest heavily in cybersecurity and identity protection programs. The psychological toll is equally significant, as victims report feelings of helplessness, fear, and anxiety that linger long after the initial theft.

Law Enforcement and Prevention

Law enforcement agencies around the world are working tirelessly to combat the trade in stolen digital lives. Operations often target major data brokers and marketplaces, seizing servers and arresting key figures. However, the global nature of the dark web and the sheer volume of stolen data make eradication nearly impossible.

Prevention, therefore, is critical. Experts recommend:

- Using strong, unique passwords and enabling two-factor authentication.
- Regularly monitoring bank statements and credit reports.
- Being cautious with unsolicited emails or suspicious links.
- Keeping devices updated with the latest security patches.
- Using VPNs and secure browsers to minimize digital footprints.

Still, no precaution can completely eliminate the risk. As long as data remains valuable and markets exist to sell it, the trade in digital lives will continue to thrive.

The sale of digital lives on the dark web underscores a sobering truth: in the digital age, our identities are as valuable as currency. Criminals do not need to steal wallets when they can steal entire lives with a few clicks. The dark web's bazaars of fullz and identity kits remind us that protecting personal data is not just about convenience—it's about survival. While law enforcement and security experts work tirelessly to fight back, individuals must also remain vigilant. In the shadows of the dark web, your digital life is a commodity waiting to be sold.

Ransomware and Exploits-as-a-Service

In recent years, the dark web has become the breeding ground for one of the most dangerous trends in cybercrime: Ransomware-as-a-Service (RaaS) and Exploits-as-a-Service (EaaS). These underground business models have fundamentally transformed the landscape of cyberattacks, lowering the barrier of entry for criminals and fueling an unprecedented surge in digital extortion and exploitation. Instead of needing advanced technical skills, even inexperienced criminals can now launch sophisticated attacks simply by renting tools from dark web vendors. This commercialization of cybercrime has made the threat more widespread, organized, and profitable than ever before.

Understanding Ransomware-as-a-Service

Ransomware is a type of malicious software that encrypts a victim's data, rendering it inaccessible until a ransom is paid—usually in cryptocurrency. Traditionally, creating and deploying ransomware required advanced hacking skills. With Ransomware-as-a-Service, however, developers design the malware and lease it to affiliates who carry out the attacks.

The RaaS model operates much like a legitimate business. Developers provide:

- Customizable ransomware kits.
- Step-by-step guides for deployment.
- Technical support and troubleshooting.
- Payment processing systems using cryptocurrencies like Bitcoin or Monero.

In exchange, the developers take a percentage of the ransom payments, often between 20–40%. The affiliates keep the rest, creating a lucrative partnership. This model allows developers to profit without directly committing the attacks themselves, while affiliates gain access to powerful malware without needing deep technical expertise.

The Mechanics of a RaaS Attack

A typical RaaS attack follows a predictable cycle:

1. **Access:** Affiliates obtain access to victims' systems through phishing emails, malicious attachments, or exploiting vulnerabilities.
2. **Deployment:** The ransomware encrypts critical files, effectively locking the victim out of their data.
3. **Ransom Demand:** Victims receive a message demanding payment in cryptocurrency in exchange for the decryption key.
4. **Payment or Consequences:** If the victim pays, they may (but not always) receive the key. If not, their data may be permanently destroyed or leaked online.

Some RaaS operators even offer "double extortion," threatening not only to withhold decryption keys but also to publicly release stolen sensitive data if the ransom is not paid.

Exploits-as-a-Service: The New Frontier

While ransomware is one of the most visible threats, Exploits-as-a-Service represents an equally dangerous evolution. In this model, cybercriminals sell or rent access to zero-day exploits (previously unknown vulnerabilities) and hacking tools. Buyers can use these exploits to compromise systems, steal data, or distribute additional malware.

EaaS marketplaces often advertise like legitimate software vendors, boasting user-friendly interfaces, reviews, and even "customer service." Prices vary depending on the sophistication and rarity of the exploit. A simple phishing kit might cost $50, while a powerful zero-day exploit can sell for thousands of dollars.

The rise of EaaS has made advanced hacking capabilities accessible to virtually anyone with money to spend, creating a flood of attacks from actors who previously lacked the skills to operate independently.

The Role of the Dark Web in Facilitating RaaS and EaaS

The dark web provides the perfect environment for these services to thrive:

- **Anonymity:** Vendors and buyers can communicate without revealing their identities.
- **Cryptocurrency Payments:** Transactions are conducted in Bitcoin or Monero, making financial trails harder to trace.

- **Bulletproof Hosting:** Services are often hosted on servers in jurisdictions unwilling to cooperate with international law enforcement.
- **Trust Systems:** Marketplaces use reputation scores, escrow services, and reviews to build trust between buyers and sellers.

This infrastructure mirrors legitimate e-commerce platforms, making the trade of illegal cyber tools disturbingly efficient and professional.

The Impact on Businesses and Individuals

The consequences of RaaS and EaaS are devastating. Businesses of all sizes have fallen victim to ransomware attacks, with losses ranging from a few thousand dollars to millions. Hospitals have had to cancel surgeries, schools have shut down for days, and local governments have been paralyzed by encrypted systems.

For individuals, ransomware can mean losing irreplaceable personal data, while exploits can lead to stolen credentials, drained bank accounts, and identity theft. The growing sophistication of these attacks ensures that no sector or person is immune.

Law Enforcement and Countermeasures

Fighting RaaS and EaaS presents unique challenges. Law enforcement agencies, including Europol, the FBI, and Interpol, have launched joint operations to identify and arrest developers and affiliates. Successful cases, such as the takedown of the REvil ransomware gang, demonstrate that these networks are vulnerable to coordinated action.

At the same time, cybersecurity firms are investing heavily in threat intelligence, creating detection systems for known ransomware strains, and developing tools to help victims recover encrypted files without paying ransoms. International collaboration remains key, as these operations often span multiple countries and legal jurisdictions.

Prevention is equally critical. Organizations are urged to:

- Regularly back up data offline.
- Use multi-factor authentication.
- Train employees to recognize phishing attempts.
- Keep systems updated with the latest security patches.
- Implement advanced endpoint detection and response systems.

The emergence of Ransomware-as-a-Service and Exploits-as-a-Service illustrates how the dark web has transformed cybercrime into a commercialized, scalable industry. By lowering the barrier to entry, these models have unleashed a wave of attacks that threaten individuals, businesses, and governments worldwide. While law enforcement continues to adapt, the battle is ongoing, and vigilance is more critical than ever. In the age of digital crime-as-a-service, the dark web has proven that anonymity and profit can be a powerful—and dangerous—combination.

Chapter 10
Dark Web Myths vs Reality

When people hear the term "dark web," their minds often race to the most horrifying possibilities: live-streamed torture sessions, hired assassins just a few clicks away, and secret marketplaces for human organs. Fueled by media reports, internet rumors, and Hollywood thrillers, these stories blur the line between truth and fiction, creating a mystique around the dark web that is both fascinating and terrifying. But how much of it is real?

The dark web has always been a breeding ground for conspiracy theories and sensational claims. Stories about “Red Rooms” where people are tortured on live camera for paying audiences, or of underground syndicates openly auctioning off human organs, have circulated for years. These narratives gain traction because they tap into our deepest fears—about technology, human cruelty, and the limits of morality when hidden behind a screen.

In this chapter, we strip away the fiction to reveal the facts. We’ll explore the origins of these myths, the psychology behind why people believe them, and whether there’s any truth buried within the horror stories. From fake hitman sites to “shock content” scams that exploit curiosity and fear, we'll uncover how criminals use fear and fantasy as tools for deception—and profit.

We'll also examine Hollywood's portrayal of the dark web and how it distorts public understanding. While the real dark web does harbor dangerous corners, it's often far less dramatic—and far more technical—than pop culture suggests. By separating fact from fear, this chapter brings clarity to the chaos and helps you understand what truly lurks beneath the surface.

Red Rooms and Hitmen: Scams or Real?

Among the most chilling legends tied to the dark web are "Red Rooms" and online hitmen-for-hire. These concepts have become a staple in horror stories, online forums, and urban legends, painting the dark web as a dystopian nightmare where unimaginable crimes are live-streamed for twisted pleasure or executed upon request with the click of a button. But how much of this is real? Are Red Rooms and assassins-for-hire actual phenomena on the dark web—or merely digital boogeymen?

The Myth of Red Rooms

The term "Red Room" refers to a supposed live-streamed broadcast—often on the dark web—where viewers can pay in cryptocurrency to watch real-time torture, abuse, or even murder. Some versions of the myth claim that the audience can vote or comment to decide what gruesome act comes next, turning the experience into a horrific game of control and depravity.

The concept gained popularity through creepypasta forums, Reddit threads, and fictional videos, often going viral and being mistaken for real events. The mystery surrounding the dark web has helped these myths flourish, as people are naturally drawn to the idea of forbidden places and unseen horrors.

However, no credible evidence has ever surfaced to prove the existence of an actual Red Room. Cybersecurity experts, journalists, and law enforcement agencies—including the FBI and Interpol—have thoroughly investigated these claims and found nothing but rumors and cleverly faked content.

Most so-called Red Rooms are hoaxes or scams. Videos found online claiming to be "live torture feeds" are typically staged, stolen from unrelated sources, or pre-recorded shock content from violent websites on the surface web. Scammers often use these terrifying myths to lure curious users or extort money under false pretenses.

The Hitman-for-Hire Scam

Hitmen-for-hire is another common narrative tied to the dark web. According to internet lore, users can simply access a .onion site, browse through profiles of contract killers, and pay in Bitcoin to have someone eliminated. These services often include pricing for different methods—poison, accident, public execution—adding a disturbing layer of professionalism to the hoax.

But again, reality doesn't match the fiction.

While there are numerous dark web sites claiming to offer assassination services, nearly all of them are scams. These sites typically use sophisticated layouts, testimonials, and even "live chat" features to convince users of their legitimacy. They ask for large upfront payments—usually in untraceable cryptocurrencies—and then vanish after receiving the money. No services are ever rendered, and no targets are harmed.

One of the most notorious examples is the Besa Mafia scam, which surfaced in 2016. The site claimed to be the largest hitman network in the world and was reportedly responsible for several murder plots. However, security researchers and law enforcement agencies eventually exposed it as an elaborate fraud. Its creator collected over $70,000 in Bitcoin before being unmasked—and no evidence of completed hits was ever found.

In fact, law enforcement agencies monitor many of these fake sites closely. In several cases, people attempting to solicit a hit have been arrested after sending payments or engaging in discussions with undercover agents posing as assassins. The irony is that those trying to hire a killer end up being the only ones committing an actual crime.

Why These Myths Persist

Despite being thoroughly debunked, Red Rooms and online hitmen remain among the most persistent dark web myths. Why?

Fear sells. These stories tap into the darkest parts of the human psyche—our curiosity about evil, our fear of losing control, and our fascination with what's forbidden. They're also amplified by media sensationalism, movies, and shows that blur the line between fiction and reality.

In addition, the technical nature of the dark web creates a barrier of entry. Most people don't access it directly, so they rely on second-hand accounts, conspiracy forums, and viral videos—which are often filled with exaggerations or outright fabrications.

The Real Danger

While Red Rooms and hitman sites may be fake, the fear they generate is rooted in real concerns. The dark web does harbor dangerous content—such as child exploitation, extremist propaganda, and stolen data. There are real harms taking place in the hidden corners of the internet, even if they don't match the horror-movie depictions.

Moreover, the scammers behind Red Rooms and hitmen-for-hire schemes are dangerous in a different way. They exploit fear and desperation for financial gain and often leave victims feeling violated or paranoid—even if the threat was never real.

Red Rooms and hitmen-for-hire are powerful symbols of the dark web's mythos—but they are, for the most part, elaborate scams and urban legends. The truth is less cinematic, but no less important: the real dangers of the dark web lie in deception, manipulation, and the exploitation of fear. Understanding what's real—and what's not—is essential for anyone seeking to explore the hidden layers of the internet responsibly.

Organ Trafficking: Urban Legend or Market?

Organ trafficking is one of the most disturbing topics associated with the dark web—an idea that strikes fear deep into the heart of anyone who hears about it. Stories have circulated online for years: shadowy websites auctioning kidneys, black-market surgeons performing transplants in back rooms, and victims waking up in bathtubs full of ice with stitches where their organs once were. These stories are widely believed, passed around as cautionary tales, and often cited as proof of the depravity hidden in the internet's darkest corners. But how much of this is grounded in truth?

The Myth

The notion of organ trafficking on the dark web is closely tied to popular culture. It appears in horror films, online creepypasta, and viral Reddit threads. Some claim to have seen sites that list organs for sale—complete with prices, photos, and donor details. Others allege that entire networks exist on .onion sites where buyers can pay for organs using cryptocurrency, often specifying the blood type or ethnicity of the donor.

This imagery is powerful—and terrifying. The idea that the human body can be disassembled and sold like merchandise is both morally horrifying and sensational enough to capture public attention. But sensational doesn't mean true.

What the Evidence Says

To date, there is no verified case of an organ being sold through a dark web marketplace. Investigations by journalists, cybersecurity researchers, and international organizations like the United Nations Office on Drugs and Crime (UNODC) have consistently failed to uncover concrete evidence of such transactions occurring online, especially in the structured way that myths suggest.

That's not to say organ trafficking doesn't happen—it does. But it primarily takes place offline, often in economically disadvantaged regions where desperate individuals are coerced or misled into selling organs. These illicit procedures are typically carried out by organized crime groups with connections in the medical industry, corrupt officials, and desperate hospitals—not anonymous online strangers communicating via Tor browser.

The logistics of organ trafficking also make the idea of "buying a kidney online" extremely implausible. Unlike drugs or credit card data, an organ cannot be simply shipped in a box. Organ transplants require exact matches, sterile conditions, time-sensitive coordination, skilled surgeons, and post-op care. These variables cannot be reliably controlled by a dark web transaction.

The Scams

Although real organ marketplaces don't exist on the dark web, scammers take full advantage of the myth. Several .onion sites claim to sell organs, often listing human hearts, kidneys, and livers with Bitcoin prices and "donor profiles." However, these sites are almost always hoaxes designed to extract money from the gullible or morbidly curious.

In some cases, users are lured in with shock content—disturbing images of bloodied bodies or medical procedures (often taken from legitimate surgical sources or crime scenes). Once engaged, visitors are asked to send cryptocurrency to reserve or bid on an organ. Of course, the site then vanishes or ceases communication once payment is received.

These scams are often part of a larger dark web ecosystem built on fear and fantasy. Like Red Rooms and hitmen-for-hire, the goal is not to provide a service but to exploit belief in horrifying possibilities for financial gain.

Real-World Organ Trafficking

While dark web organ markets are fantasy, real-world organ trafficking is tragically very real. Victims are often poor, uneducated, and unaware of the full consequences of donating an organ. They may be promised money they never receive or forced into surgery against their will. The organs are then sold to wealthier patients in need of transplants—sometimes across borders, in violation of international laws and ethics.

Some infamous cases have involved international organ trafficking rings operating in countries like India, Pakistan, Egypt, and China. These operations are typically exposed through law enforcement or whistleblower testimony—not digital traces left on the dark web.

Organizations such as the World Health Organization (WHO) and Interpol actively work to combat organ trafficking through global monitoring, education, and legal reform. But they also emphasize that most of these crimes occur through physical networks and corrupt institutions, not anonymous online deals.

Why the Myth Persists

Like many dark web myths, organ trafficking endures because it resonates on a deep emotional level. It speaks to our fear of being violated, our fascination with the body as currency, and our dread of the unknown. The concept also serves as a modern horror story—a metaphor for how dehumanizing and transactional the world can feel in the digital age.

In some ways, the myth persists because it seems just believable enough to be true. After all, the dark web has hosted marketplaces for drugs, weapons, and stolen data—why not organs? But this logic overlooks the critical differences in logistics, legality, and technology that make selling an organ far more complex than shipping a package.

Organ trafficking is a grim reality in many parts of the world—but it's not happening in the way dark web myths would have us believe. There is no verified evidence that organs are being bought or sold via Tor-based websites. What exists instead are scams, staged content, and horror stories meant to exploit fear for profit.

By understanding the difference between sensationalism and reality, we can focus on the real fight against organ trafficking—supporting vulnerable communities, enforcing medical ethics, and dismantling offline criminal networks. The dark web may be many things, but in this case, it's more shadow than substance.

What Hollywood Gets Wrong

When it comes to the dark web, Hollywood has played a significant role in shaping the public's imagination—usually in the most exaggerated, stylized, and fear-inducing ways possible. Films, television shows, and streaming dramas have presented the dark web as a sinister, chaotic underworld ruled by hackers, assassins, pedophiles, and tech-savvy villains capable of wreaking havoc with a few keystrokes. While these depictions make for thrilling entertainment, they often miss the mark—distorting both the capabilities and limitations of the dark web.

The Stereotype of the Hacker-God

One of the most common Hollywood tropes is the "super hacker"—a lone genius who can access any system, disable security grids, drain bank accounts, and break into the Pentagon with ease, all while sipping coffee in a dimly lit room. The dark web, in these stories, is portrayed as a digital jungle gym for such characters, where everything illegal and dangerous is just a few clicks away.

In reality, hacking—especially on the dark web—is far more complex, tedious, and time-consuming. Cybercriminals often rely on social engineering, phishing schemes, and malware—not flashy, cinematic hacks. Moreover, very few individuals have the expertise to both operate on the dark web securely and execute large-scale hacks. Hollywood condenses years of experience into seconds of action, giving audiences a completely unrealistic view of how online crime functions.

Red Rooms and Live Murders

Movies and TV shows love the idea of live-streamed torture chambers—so-called "Red Rooms"—where wealthy viewers pay to watch heinous crimes. While this makes for chilling horror sequences, as discussed earlier, there is no verified evidence that such Red Rooms exist. Hollywood has borrowed heavily from internet urban legends, embellishing them to elicit shock and fear.

These scenes feed into the mythos of the dark web as a place of pure evil, where morality is erased and the audience is complicit in the violence. But these portrayals ignore the technical, ethical, and logistical challenges of broadcasting high-quality, real-time video over Tor—something the network simply isn't built for. Tor is slow, encrypted, and not designed to handle streaming media efficiently, making these depictions mostly fiction.

The Instant Marketplace

Another Hollywood error is the depiction of dark web markets as easily accessible, slickly designed platforms—like Amazon for criminals. In reality, dark web marketplaces are hard to find, often require invitations or vetting, and are frequently under surveillance or taken down by law enforcement. They're not plug-and-play storefronts, but complex, volatile platforms riddled with scams, phishing pages, and exit fraud.

Additionally, films rarely show the role of cryptocurrency wallets, encryption keys, PGP messages, and other technical barriers that prevent just anyone from navigating these markets. Hollywood often skips over these elements to simplify the narrative, but in doing so, they give the impression that anyone with a Tor browser can become a drug lord or cybercriminal in five minutes.

The Anonymous Assassin

A frequent plotline involves hiring an assassin, kidnapper, or criminal through the dark web. Whether it's a scene of someone ordering a hit through a .onion site or browsing a catalog of nefarious services, the concept is deeply rooted in fiction. These services are either outright scams or sting operations run by law enforcement. There are no verified cases of successful, structured hitman-for-hire platforms operating on the dark web, despite what thrillers would have us believe.

Hollywood dramatizes this idea for maximum impact, but it overlooks the real-world motivations of dark web users. Most users are more interested in anonymity, whistleblowing, or illicit commerce—not cinematic acts of violence.

Visual Aesthetic vs. Reality

Visually, the dark web is often portrayed as an otherworldly space filled with glitchy animations, green matrix code, and spinning skulls. In truth, most dark web sites are bare-bones and outdated-looking. They're primarily text-based, clunky, and lack the sleek design seen in surface web platforms. The dark web isn't a digital haunted house—it's more like a dimly lit library with broken links, poor UI, and a lot of repetition.

This visual disconnect adds to the mystique and fear. The less people know about the dark web, the easier it is for Hollywood to sell the idea of a twisted, hellish online environment.

Why It Matters

While it's easy to dismiss these portrayals as "just entertainment," they can have real-world consequences. By sensationalizing and mythologizing the dark web, Hollywood contributes to public fear, misinformation, and digital illiteracy. People may either overestimate the dark web's danger or underestimate its complexity—both of which can lead to poor decisions.

These depictions also affect law enforcement narratives, policy development, and public funding. When fear outweighs facts, we risk misunderstanding how the dark web actually works—and how it might be used for both harm and good.

Hollywood has taken the dark web and turned it into a dystopian nightmare playground for villains and victims alike. While this has entertained millions, it has also clouded the public's understanding of what the dark web truly is. The truth is more nuanced, more technical, and far less theatrical. By separating fact from fiction, we can better navigate the real risks and opportunities within the hidden layers of the internet—and avoid falling for the smoke and mirrors crafted for the silver screen.

Chapter 11
Staying Safe in a Digital World

In an era where nearly every aspect of our lives is digitized, from personal communication and financial transactions to professional data and even our health records, maintaining digital security has never been more essential. The allure of the dark web, with its layers of secrecy and promise of anonymity, often attracts the curious, the cautious, and the criminal alike. But what many don't realize is that simply exploring these hidden corners of the internet—even with good intentions—can expose users to serious risks. Identity theft, malware attacks, phishing schemes, and surveillance are just the beginning.

Chapter 11 shines a light on the protective measures everyone should understand before venturing into the shadows. It starts by examining how to safeguard your identity and digital devices—not only from cybercriminals but also from the many traps that exist within the dark web itself. Just as you wouldn't walk into an unfamiliar city without a map, you shouldn't navigate the dark web without robust cybersecurity tools and a clear understanding of the terrain.

We'll explore the roles of VPNs, Tor browsers, and encryption, breaking down how they work, what they protect, and where their limits lie. These technologies are powerful shields when used correctly—but they are not magic cloaks. Missteps can turn anonymity into exposure.

Finally, we'll address the psychological trap of curiosity. Many users are drawn into the dark web thinking it's a harmless adventure or a place to "just look around." But this curiosity, when uninformed, can quickly lead to dangerous consequences.

This chapter isn't just about technology—it's about mindset, responsibility, and recognizing that safety in the digital world requires more than good software. It requires awareness, preparation, and a healthy respect for the invisible threats lurking behind the screen.

Protecting Your Identity and Devices

In today's hyper-connected world, protecting your identity and digital devices isn't just a recommendation—it's a necessity. With the growing threat of cybercrime and the increasing ease of accessing risky online spaces like the dark web, the line between curiosity and vulnerability is thinner than ever. Whether you're a casual browser, a researcher, or a whistleblower, safeguarding your digital presence is your first defense against identity theft, malware, surveillance, and other online dangers.

Understanding the Risks

Before diving into tools and strategies, it's important to understand what's at stake. Your digital identity includes more than your name and email—it encompasses your IP address, browsing habits, stored credentials, biometric data, device metadata, and even your behavioral patterns online. Any one of these can be used to profile you, steal your identity, or launch targeted attacks.

Hackers and malicious actors thrive on exploiting weak security. They use phishing attacks to lure victims into sharing personal details, deploy keyloggers to capture passwords, and even exploit vulnerabilities in outdated software to access entire systems. The dark web, in particular, is rife with these traps—often hidden within seemingly innocuous links or downloads.

Strong Password Practices

The first layer of defense is simple but often overlooked: strong, unique passwords. Avoid using the same password across multiple platforms. Use a mix of uppercase and lowercase letters, numbers, and special characters. Password managers like Bitwarden, 1Password, or LastPass can help you generate and store complex passwords securely.

Two-factor authentication (2FA) adds an extra shield. Even if your password is compromised, the attacker would need access to your secondary authentication method—often a code sent to your phone or generated by an authenticator app.

Keep Software Updated

Security vulnerabilities are often found in outdated software. Make it a habit to regularly update your operating system, browser, antivirus software, and any applications you use. Enable automatic updates wherever possible. Cybercriminals often exploit known flaws in unpatched systems—known as zero-day vulnerabilities—to gain access to your data.

Use Reliable Antivirus and Anti-Malware Tools

Install reputable antivirus and anti-malware software and keep it updated. These programs can detect, quarantine, and remove malicious code before it causes harm. Premium security suites often include firewall protection, real-time scanning, and web filters that warn you before visiting suspicious sites.

Securing Your Network

Your internet connection is a gateway to your digital life. If you're using public Wi-Fi—whether in a coffee shop, airport, or hotel—you're putting your data at risk. Public networks are often unencrypted, making it easy for hackers to intercept your communications.

To minimize risk:

- Avoid logging into sensitive accounts on public Wi-Fi.
- Use a virtual private network (VPN) to encrypt your connection and hide your IP address.
- Change default router passwords at home and ensure your network uses strong WPA3 encryption.

Protecting Your Devices

Your smartphone, tablet, and computer store enormous amounts of personal data. If stolen or compromised, they become a treasure trove for cybercriminals.

To secure your devices:

- **Enable full-disk encryption** (like FileVault for Mac or BitLocker for Windows).

- **Use biometric locks or strong PINs** instead of simple patterns or easy-to-guess codes.
- **Disable Bluetooth, AirDrop, or file-sharing options** when not in use.
- **Install tracking and remote wipe software** in case your device is lost or stolen.

Be Mindful of Your Digital Footprint

Every search, click, and post contributes to your digital footprint. Oversharing on social media or using unsecured websites can unintentionally expose sensitive details.

Tips to reduce your exposure:

- Use privacy-focused search engines like DuckDuckGo or Startpage.
- Limit what you share online, especially location-based information.
- Regularly review the permissions you grant apps and browser extensions.

Safe Browsing Habits

If you're exploring deeper layers of the web, caution is paramount. Many sites on the dark web host malware or lead to phishing attempts.

Always:

- Avoid downloading unknown files or clicking suspicious links.
- Verify URLs carefully, especially on .onion sites.
- Do not input personal information anywhere on the dark web.

- Use the Tor browser carefully, with scripts and JavaScript disabled when possible.

Back Up Your Data

Even with all precautions, breaches can still occur. Regularly backing up your data—using both local and cloud solutions—can save you in case of a ransomware attack, hardware failure, or accidental deletion. Encrypt your backups and store them in a secure location.

Cybersecurity isn't a one-time task—it's a continuous mindset. By taking steps to protect your identity and devices, you're not only shielding yourself from cyber threats but also setting a foundation of digital resilience. Whether you're a casual user or someone operating in high-risk online environments, these best practices create a barrier between you and those who seek to exploit your digital presence. In the shadows of the internet, awareness is your greatest armor.

The Role of VPNs, Tor, and Encryption

In an increasingly digital age, where surveillance, data collection, and cyber threats lurk behind every click, privacy-focused tools have become essential for safeguarding individual rights. Among the most powerful of these tools are VPNs (Virtual Private Networks), the Tor browser, and various forms of encryption. Each serves a unique purpose, but when used together, they form a layered defense that protects identity, communication, and data from prying eyes.

What is a VPN?

A Virtual Private Network (VPN) acts as a secure tunnel between your device and the internet. When you connect to a VPN, your internet traffic is rerouted through an encrypted server, masking your real IP address and hiding your online activities from Internet Service Providers (ISPs), governments, and potential attackers.

For example, if you're in Pakistan and connect to a VPN server in Germany, your browsing activity appears to originate from Germany. This makes it difficult for third parties to trace your online movements or track your identity.

Key Benefits of VPNs:

- Masking of IP address for anonymity.
- Protection from Wi-Fi snooping on public networks.
- Bypassing geo-restrictions and censorship.
- Avoidance of tracking by ISPs or advertisers.

However, it's important to choose a trustworthy VPN provider. Avoid free VPNs, as many have been caught logging user data or injecting ads. Look for VPNs with a no-logs policy, strong encryption standards (like AES-256), and independent audits. Examples of reliable providers include NordVPN, ExpressVPN, ProtonVPN, and Mullvad.

What is Tor?

Tor (The Onion Router) is a browser and network system designed specifically for anonymity. It works by routing your internet traffic through a series of volunteer-operated servers called nodes or relays. Each relay removes a layer of encryption (like peeling an onion), ensuring that no single point knows both who you are and what you're doing.

The Tor browser is the most common way to access this network. It allows users to:

- Browse anonymously.
- Access .onion websites (which are only available on the dark web).
- Bypass censorship in authoritarian regions.

Unlike VPNs, which protect traffic from your device to a specific VPN server, Tor provides anonymity across a distributed network. However, because your traffic passes through multiple relays, the connection is typically slower. Tor also disables many browser features by default (such as JavaScript and certain plugins) to prevent tracking.

Tor Best Practices:

- Never use your real name or personal email while browsing through Tor.
- Avoid logging into accounts that reveal your identity.
- Don't maximize the browser window—it can fingerprint your device.
- Never download files through Tor without proper sandboxing, as this can expose your IP address.

Tor is a critical tool for journalists, activists, and researchers who require anonymity. But it's also used by malicious actors, which contributes to the stigma surrounding it.

Encryption: The Invisible Armor

Encryption is the foundation of digital privacy. At its core, encryption transforms data into a coded format that only authorized parties can decode. It ensures that even if your data is intercepted, it cannot be read without the correct decryption key.

There are two main types of encryption:

- **Symmetric Encryption:** The same key is used to encrypt and decrypt data.
- **Asymmetric Encryption:** A public key encrypts data, while a private key decrypts it (used in secure messaging and emails).

Applications of Encryption:

- **HTTPS** websites use SSL/TLS encryption to protect web traffic.
- **Messaging apps** like Signal, WhatsApp, and Telegram use end-to-end encryption, meaning only you and the recipient can read the messages.
- **Encrypted file storage** services like Tresorit or ProtonDrive protect your stored data.
- **PGP (Pretty Good Privacy)** is used to encrypt emails, files, and communication for advanced users.

VPN + Tor + Encryption: A Powerful Combination

Each of these tools has strengths and weaknesses. But together, they create a robust security framework.

- **VPN + Tor:** By connecting to a VPN before opening the Tor browser, you hide Tor usage from your ISP and gain an additional layer of protection. This method is known as Tor over VPN.

- **Encryption + VPN:** Even if your VPN connection is compromised, local file or message encryption keeps your sensitive data safe.
- **Tor + Encryption:** If you're communicating with someone over the Tor network using an encrypted messaging app like Signal, your conversation is doubly protected—from both traffic analysis and message decryption.

The Limits of Technology

While these tools are powerful, they are not foolproof. Mistakes—such as logging into real accounts, downloading files, or sharing identifying information—can still compromise your privacy. Similarly, law enforcement agencies and surveillance bodies continuously adapt, using traffic analysis, malware implants, and zero-day exploits to unmask users.

Staying safe in a digital world is as much about habits and discipline as it is about technology. No tool can protect a careless user.

Why Curiosity Can Be Dangerous

In a world increasingly defined by digital connectivity, the allure of the unknown is stronger than ever. The internet has long been a double-edged sword: a source of vast knowledge and creativity on one side, and a gateway to risk and darkness on the other. Among the most tempting rabbit holes is the dark web, a space cloaked in anonymity, controversy, and mystery. For many, a simple spark of curiosity—"What's really out there?"—can become a perilous journey with unexpected consequences. In digital spaces, curiosity isn't just dangerous—it can be disastrous.

Curiosity as a Gateway

Most people don't access the dark web with malicious intent. They may be students, journalists, or tech enthusiasts curious about what lies beyond the "normal" internet. The problem is that unlike the surface web—where Google filters most threats and laws are more easily enforced—the dark web is a largely unregulated and unpredictable environment. What might start as an innocent exploration can quickly turn into an encounter with illegal marketplaces, exploitative content, or dangerous individuals.

Simply visiting certain .onion sites may unknowingly expose you to malware, surveillance traps, or law enforcement honeypots. Some websites use browser vulnerabilities or scripts to exploit visitors automatically. One wrong click is all it takes to compromise your system—or your identity.

Legal Grey Areas and Black Holes

One of the most dangerous aspects of curiosity on the dark web is how easily users can stumble into illegal territory. A link that claims to host whistleblower content might redirect to a marketplace selling drugs or weapons. Viewing or downloading illegal content—even unknowingly—is a criminal offense in many countries. And ignorance of the law is not a valid defense in court.

Moreover, just being associated with certain domains, even as a passive visitor, can raise red flags with cybersecurity agencies. Law enforcement agencies around the world monitor Tor traffic and maintain watchlists of suspicious activity. Even if you never interact with illegal content, your IP being linked to a specific access point could invite scrutiny.

The Psychological Toll

There is also a mental and emotional risk that comes with diving into the dark web. Many users report encountering deeply disturbing content—from forums that glorify violence and abuse to graphic images and unethical experiments. Exposure to this kind of material, especially without preparation or proper mental resilience, can lead to trauma, anxiety, depression, or paranoia.

For those who explore out of morbid fascination or boredom, the cost can be psychological disillusionment—realizing that some corners of the internet reflect the worst of humanity. The idea that "some things cannot be unseen" is profoundly true in this context.

Trust Is a Dangerous Illusion

Curiosity can also lead to misplaced trust. The dark web is filled with scammers, hackers, and predators who capitalize on the naivety of newcomers. You might receive messages claiming to offer rare information, anonymous friendship, or insider access—only to fall into a social engineering trap.

Many scammers disguise malware as PDF files or ZIP archives. Some pretend to run legitimate forums or offer guidance to help "new users." Once you download a file, open a message, or install a tool without knowing the source, you're potentially giving someone control over your system.

In some cases, users who think they are engaging in private conversations on encrypted platforms are actually talking to undercover agents or intelligence bots collecting data.

You Leave a Trail

Many people assume that because the dark web is "anonymous," they are invisible. This is a myth. While tools like Tor and VPNs mask your identity to a degree, you still leave behind metadata, timing patterns, and behavioral fingerprints. Law enforcement agencies and skilled hackers can piece these together—especially if you make one small mistake, such as logging into a personal email or using an identifiable alias.

Once your data is compromised, it can be sold, misused, or even weaponized against you.

Curiosity Without Preparation

There is a difference between informed exploration and reckless curiosity. The dark web is not a playground—it's more like a minefield. Venturing in without understanding how to protect yourself is like wandering into a war zone blindfolded.

Before even considering exploring the dark web, one must:

- Understand the technology (Tor, VPNs, encryption).
- Harden their system against vulnerabilities.
- Know the laws in their jurisdiction.
- Have a clear purpose and exit strategy.
- Be mentally prepared for what they may encounter.

Otherwise, curiosity becomes a loaded weapon—one you may accidentally fire at yourself.

When Not Knowing Is Safer

While curiosity drives innovation, creativity, and discovery, it must be tempered with caution, especially in the digital realm. The dark web is not inherently evil, but it is undeniably dangerous—especially to the unprepared. The thrill of exploration is never worth sacrificing your safety, freedom, or peace of mind.

Sometimes, the safest path is to respect the warning signs and stay away from the shadows—no matter how curious you are.

Chapter 12
The Future of the Dark Web

The dark web, long shrouded in mystery and controversy, is not a static space—it evolves as rapidly as the technologies that shape it. What began as a U.S. Navy research project has morphed into a decentralized, encrypted ecosystem used by whistleblowers, criminals, dissidents, and everyday users seeking anonymity. As we stand at the crossroads of emerging technologies like artificial intelligence (AI) and blockchain, the question arises: what will the dark web become in the coming decade?

This final chapter explores the road ahead. From the growing use of AI to automate both cybercrime and cybersecurity, to the rise of decentralized platforms that promise even greater anonymity, we examine how innovation is redefining both the power and peril of the dark web. Blockchain technology, often celebrated for powering cryptocurrencies, may also serve as the foundation for anonymous identity management, uncensorable publishing, and decentralized marketplaces that operate far beyond government oversight.

At the same time, state actors are not sitting idle. Governments are deploying sophisticated surveillance tools, machine learning models, and international alliances to unmask users and dismantle dark web operations. This tug-of-war between privacy rights and national security is intensifying, prompting serious ethical and legal questions about the future of internet freedom.

In this final exploration, we ask: Can anonymity survive in a world obsessed with transparency and control? Is the dark web destined to shrink under the weight of regulation and surveillance—or will it adapt and expand into something even more elusive?

The future of the dark web is not just a technological question—it's a societal one. And what happens next may determine the shape of digital freedom for generations to come.

AI, Blockchain, and the Evolution of Anonymity

The dark web has always been a battleground between those seeking anonymity and those seeking control. At its core lies a fundamental tension: the right to privacy versus the need for accountability. As we move into a future shaped by rapid advancements in technology, two innovations are dramatically transforming this landscape—artificial intelligence (AI) and blockchain. Together, they are redefining how anonymity is achieved, protected, and potentially exploited.

Artificial Intelligence: A Double-Edged Sword

AI has become a powerful force in both cyber-defense and cybercrime. On the one hand, governments and law enforcement agencies are using AI-driven tools to unmask hidden identities, detect behavioral patterns, and monitor dark web activity in real time. Machine learning algorithms can now scan vast amounts of encrypted data to flag suspicious behaviors, such as transactions that resemble money laundering or marketplace listings involving illicit goods.

Facial recognition tools, natural language processing (NLP), and predictive analytics are also being deployed to identify users operating under multiple aliases. In essence, AI is steadily eroding the veil of anonymity that once protected users of the dark web.

However, AI is not just a surveillance tool. It's also being adopted by cybercriminals. Malicious actors are training AI models to craft more convincing phishing attacks, generate deepfake videos, and automate identity theft. Some even use generative AI to build fake storefronts and scam websites on dark web marketplaces—replicating legitimate platforms to deceive users. In forums where anonymity is king, AI helps users mask their linguistic style and writing habits, making them harder to track across platforms.

In the hands of the wrong people, AI is a powerful weapon for deception and scale. In the hands of defenders, it's a tool for precision and early detection. This arms race is likely to intensify in the coming years.

Blockchain: Trust in a Trustless World

Where AI brings automation, blockchain brings decentralization. Its most well-known application, cryptocurrency, has already transformed the dark web by enabling anonymous payments. Bitcoin and Monero are frequently used in transactions involving drugs, weapons, data, and other contraband. But blockchain's role is evolving beyond just digital currency.

Emerging blockchain technologies are enabling the development of decentralized identity (DID) systems. These allow users to create self-sovereign identities that are not tied to a central authority. In theory, a person could prove their identity or credentials—like age, nationality, or professional status—without revealing personal information. On the dark web, this could mean buyers and sellers verifying each other's credibility without ever sharing real-world data.

Moreover, decentralized marketplaces are rising. Unlike traditional dark net markets, which rely on centralized administrators (and are therefore vulnerable to shutdowns and scams), decentralized markets run on smart contracts—automated scripts stored on a blockchain that execute transactions without human intervention. These markets are harder to dismantle, and they increase the resilience of illicit economies.

Blockchain is also enabling censorship-resistant publishing. Platforms like IPFS (InterPlanetary File System) and Arweave allow users to store and distribute content permanently without the fear of takedown. This is a double-edged sword: while it empowers whistleblowers and journalists under authoritarian regimes, it also means that harmful content, once published, could become impossible to erase.

A New Model of Anonymity

Together, AI and blockchain are shaping a new model of anonymity—one that is smarter, more adaptive, and increasingly decentralized. Rather than simply hiding identities, future anonymity may revolve around verifiable trust: proving you are a legitimate user without disclosing who you are. Blockchain-based zero-knowledge proofs and decentralized identifiers could allow for this level of selective disclosure.

Meanwhile, AI could be used to enhance user safety by detecting scams and malware in real-time—even on anonymous platforms. Imagine a system where your dark web browser warns you before entering a phishing site, or flags suspicious code in a file you're about to download. These tools would preserve privacy while reducing risk.

Of course, these benefits are not guaranteed. If governments monopolize AI tools and regulate blockchain use too heavily, the balance may shift towards surveillance and control. On the flip side, if criminals fully harness these technologies first, the dark web could become even more dangerous and impenetrable than it is today.

The Unwritten Future

As we look ahead, one thing is certain: anonymity will not disappear—it will evolve. AI and blockchain are shaping the contours of a new digital underground, where identity is fluid, trust is programmable, and surveillance is omnipresent. Whether this future is empowering or dystopian depends on how these tools are governed, who controls them, and how society adapts to the ethical questions they raise.

In the coming decade, the struggle between privacy and power will be waged not just in courtrooms or governments—but in code, algorithms, and decentralized networks. And the dark web, once considered a fringe corner of the internet, may well be its most telling battleground.

Government Surveillance vs Privacy Rights

As the digital landscape grows more complex, so does the battle between privacy advocates and government surveillance operations. The dark web, once a niche space for privacy-seeking technologists, now sits squarely at the heart of a global debate: how much privacy should individuals be allowed in an increasingly interconnected world? And at what point does that privacy become a threat to public safety?

The Expanding Eye of the State

Governments across the world—especially in developed nations—are pouring billions into surveillance infrastructure. Agencies like the NSA (National Security Agency) in the United States, GCHQ (Government Communications Headquarters) in the United Kingdom, and similar entities in China, Russia, and India have developed vast digital surveillance capabilities. These range from bulk metadata collection and real-time traffic monitoring to advanced AI tools that scan for suspicious patterns on the surface web and within encrypted spaces like the dark web.

These agencies argue that such measures are essential for national security. In the post-9/11 era, and even more so following the rise of cyberterrorism and foreign influence campaigns, the justification for broad surveillance powers has gained traction. Monitoring the dark web is seen as necessary to track illegal arms trades, prevent terrorist recruitment, combat child exploitation, and intercept criminal communications.

However, this mission is complicated by the fact that the very technologies used to mask identity—Tor, encryption, decentralized platforms—are also used by human rights defenders, political dissidents, and whistleblowers. Surveillance programs that seek to break or bypass these protections can easily spill over into broader rights violations.

The Chilling Effect

One of the most concerning aspects of mass surveillance is the chilling effect—the tendency for individuals to self-censor or limit their behavior when they know they're being watched. This psychological impact can erode freedom of expression, even among those who are not breaking any laws.

For instance, journalists investigating sensitive topics—such as corruption, corporate misconduct, or military operations—may be discouraged from using secure digital channels for fear of being flagged or targeted. In authoritarian regimes, this fear is not just hypothetical; it is enforced through imprisonment, censorship, and violence.

Even in democratic nations, surveillance has begun to blur ethical lines. Revelations by whistleblowers like Edward Snowden exposed how the NSA operated expansive programs like PRISM, which collected data from major tech companies without users' consent. The backlash was fierce, prompting legal challenges, transparency campaigns, and calls for reforms. But the surveillance apparatus has continued to grow, often in secret, and with limited oversight.

Privacy as a Human Right

Privacy is enshrined in various international declarations and constitutions as a fundamental human right. The United Nations recognizes the right to privacy in the digital age under Article 12 of the Universal Declaration of Human Rights. The European Union has taken a firm stance with its General Data Protection Regulation (GDPR), reinforcing individuals' control over their digital data.

Despite these protections, the rise of surveillance capitalism—where private companies track, analyze, and sell user data—and government overreach presents a grave threat to individual autonomy. The dark web, in this context, has become a last refuge for people who want to maintain control over their identities, their communications, and their digital footprints.

Tools like encrypted email, Tor, and decentralized messaging platforms are used not only by criminals but also by lawyers, activists, NGOs, and average citizens wary of prying eyes. The right to digital privacy is not a luxury—it is a modern necessity.

The Push for Backdoors

One of the most contentious issues in this debate is the demand for "backdoors" in encrypted systems. Governments have repeatedly called on tech companies to build secret access points that allow law enforcement to bypass encryption under specific conditions. Proponents argue this would enable authorities to investigate and stop serious crimes faster.

However, security experts warn that any backdoor is a vulnerability, and once created, it can be exploited by malicious actors, foreign governments, or even insiders. Encryption, by design, is meant to be mathematically unbreakable. Weakening it—even with good intentions—endangers everyone.

Tech companies, civil liberties groups, and cybersecurity professionals have largely opposed these demands, stating that strong encryption protects global commerce, democratic discourse, and personal safety in an age of digital threats.

Finding Balance in the Digital Age

The challenge moving forward is to find a sustainable balance between surveillance and privacy. Democracies must be transparent about the scope and limits of their surveillance activities, ensuring that oversight mechanisms are robust and independent. At the same time, there must be open dialogue about the risks of unregulated anonymity and the responsibility of users.

Education plays a pivotal role. When users understand how data is collected, where it goes, and who has access to it, they are better equipped to make informed decisions about the tools they use and the spaces they explore—be it on the surface web or the darkest corners of the internet.

The future of the dark web is deeply tied to this global reckoning. Surveillance will grow smarter. Privacy tools will evolve in response. The outcome depends on how we, as a society, choose to define the limits of power, and how fiercely we defend the right to disappear when we need to.

What Happens Next?

The dark web, once relegated to the outer fringes of internet culture, now stands at the intersection of some of the most pressing global questions—privacy vs. surveillance, freedom vs. regulation, decentralization vs. control. As we move forward into an increasingly digital world, the role of the dark web will not diminish; instead, it will evolve, adapt, and likely grow more influential, more elusive, and more debated than ever before.

A Shifting Landscape

The dark web is no longer a static ecosystem hidden beneath layers of code. It is a dynamic, morphing landscape shaped by politics, innovation, and human behavior. With the rise of censorship in many parts of the world, people are turning to hidden networks to communicate freely, share restricted information, and organize resistance. Simultaneously, criminal networks are refining their operations, leveraging advanced tools like cryptocurrencies, AI-generated identities, and private blockchains to stay ahead of law enforcement.

What happens next is not solely about technology—it's about how governments, individuals, and global communities respond to the fundamental issues of trust, access, control, and ethical use.

The Push for Regulation

Governments across the globe are stepping up efforts to regulate the web, including the dark web. New cybercrime legislation, cross-border data-sharing alliances, and digital identity initiatives are already in development. For example, the European Union's Digital Services Act and Digital Markets Act aim to create a safer, more transparent digital space. Other countries are discussing mandatory know-your-customer (KYC) standards for crypto transactions and imposing stricter oversight on encrypted platforms.

If these measures continue, we may witness a gradual narrowing of what is possible on the open web. This, in turn, may push even more users toward the dark web—not just for criminal activity, but as a means of escaping increasingly controlled environments. Paradoxically, over-regulation may serve to empower the very system it seeks to suppress.

Technological Arms Race

As law enforcement becomes more tech-savvy—deploying AI for behavioral analysis, machine learning for detecting patterns, and blockchain tracking tools—users of the dark web will continue to find new ways to stay hidden. Quantum computing, for example, could eventually break current encryption standards, posing a major threat to both cybersecurity and privacy alike. On the flip side, post-quantum cryptography is already being developed to defend against that future threat.

Additionally, decentralized autonomous organizations (DAOs) and anonymous decentralized storage systems are gaining popularity. These innovations may birth entire internet ecosystems that exist outside any traditional regulatory framework—completely peer-to-peer, encrypted, and resistant to takedown. In this reality, the dark web may simply become one node in a much larger, more fragmented digital underground.

Rise of Ethical Use Cases

It's important to recognize that not all future developments are dystopian. The dark web has long served as a platform for good—used by whistleblowers, investigative journalists, political dissidents, and oppressed communities. As authoritarianism grows in some regions, the demand for censorship-resistant platforms will increase.

More developers are focusing on ethical anonymity—creating tools that allow people to remain private without enabling harm. Future platforms may include built-in safeguards such as community reporting, decentralized arbitration, and smart contract limitations to prevent abuse while preserving user protection.

Projects like SecureDrop, used by major news outlets to receive confidential information, are early examples of how the dark web's infrastructure can support transparency and justice.

Education and Awareness

One of the most critical developments in the coming years will be digital education. As more people become aware of their digital footprints and the risks of online exposure, we will likely see a cultural shift in how privacy is viewed. The stigma attached to privacy-seeking behavior may begin to fade, replaced by a new understanding of privacy as a form of empowerment, not guilt.

Educational campaigns, public service tools, and even school curricula may eventually include information on digital rights, responsible encryption use, and how to spot online manipulation and scams—both on the surface web and in hidden layers.

The Ethical Crossroads

In the end, the future of the dark web will be defined not just by what's possible technologically, but by what we choose to tolerate, what we choose to protect, and what lines we refuse to cross. Will we build systems that enable freedom of speech while guarding against harm? Will we enforce privacy rights without opening the door to unchecked criminality? Will we educate future generations or let them drift into the digital shadows uninformed?

There are no easy answers, but one thing is clear: the dark web is not going away. It is evolving with us—reflecting our fears, our ideals, and our contradictions. What happens next will depend on how well we navigate that mirror.

As with any powerful tool, the dark web can be wielded for good or for evil. The responsibility lies with us—not just to monitor it, but to understand it, shape it, and prepare for the realities it continues to reveal.

www.ingramcontent.com/pod-product-compliance
Lightning Source LLC
Chambersburg PA
CBHW041259210926
51847CB00009B/80
9789699092145